Partnerships for Prosperity:
Museums and Economic Development

Partnerships for Prosperity

Museums and Economic Development

Peggy Wireman, Ph.D.

Produced Under the Auspices of
The State Historical Society of Wisconsin, Madison

Partially Funded by
A National Technical Assistance Grant from the Economic
Development Administration, U.S. Department of Commerce

Published by
The American Association of Museums, Washington, D.C.

Printed in the United States of America

The opinions in this book are those of the author, and are not to be taken as representing the views of any institution or organization, including the American Association of Museums.

Library of Congress Cataloging—in—Publication Data

Wireman, Peggy.
 Partnerships for prosperity : museums and economic development / Peggy Wireman.
   p. cm.
 "Produced under the auspices of the State Historical Society of Wisconsin, Madison; partially funded by a National Technical Assistance Grant from the Economic Development Administration, U.S. Department of Commerce."
 Includes bibliographical references.
 ISBN 0-931201-39-X (paper)
 1. Museums—United States—Management. 2. Museum finance—United States. 3. Economic Development. 4. Strategic alliances (Business)—United States. 5. Partnerships—United States. 6. Corporate sponsorship—United States. I. Title.
AM11.W57 1997
069.2—DC21   97-11411
                  CIP

Peggy Wireman, president, Wireman & Associates, is a consultant who specializes in community and economic development. Previously, she headed the Wisconsin Small Business Development Center, administered a national economic development grants program for the U.S. Department of Commerce, and taught community development at the University of Missouri. She holds a B.A. and an M.A. in American history, and a Ph.D. in sociology. She has written a book about urban neighborhoods as well as several articles. Dr. Wireman has served as a consultant in cultural tourism, small business development, and community development in the United States and in developing nations. She has visited more than 300 museums and historic sites in over 30 countries. She lives in Madison, Wis.

Contents

Our heritage has become a very public commodity that is traded openly in the marketplace. State tourism offices understand that apart from visits to relatives, scenic and historic sites make up the single largest factor affecting Americans' leisure travel decisions. The National Trust for Historic Preservation's Main Street Program, at work in over 1,000 cities in 35 states, has demonstrated that historic preservation—building on the heritage that makes each city distinctive—has become the best strategy to revitalize downtown areas. Preservation spurs investment, new business formation, job creation, and an expanded tax base. The "new urbanism" predicates its planning on historical concepts and patterns of neighborhood. Heritage and cultural organizations have become an essential part of sustainable economic development.

Among cultural organizations, the museum has become a primary place where the public comes together with history, science, and art. Diverse affinity and interest groups, as well as other "communities," have learned that the manner of presentation of their past and the interpretation of their heritage have serious consequences for the present. As such, museums are far too important to remain on the periphery of policy development and many other aspects of community activity.

Just as the "economic development types," more often than not, overlook museums as important assets in their work, museum staff too rarely see themselves as key players in those efforts. The paths that take both community developers and museum professionals to their positions rarely intersect. Smaller museums usually recruit leaders from folks trained to understand artifacts and their care, or from education, art history, or related disciplines. These museums often do not have staff dedicated to public relations, fund raising, tourism, marketing, economic development, special events, or other functions that relate directly to community promotion and development activities. Conversely, few community economic "movers and shakers" have much experience with art, artifacts, exhibits, and other common museum work.

This manual argues that, for a variety of mutually supportive reasons, the two spheres must come together. And it suggests that museums take the initiative in developing a more effective integration with economic and community development. In a very accessible style, it provides rational, practical advice, workable ideas, and examples. Museum directors and staff, trustees, and volunteers will find a common sense guide to making their institutions a more vital, important part of their community.

Those of us close to museums understand the great value of collecting, preserving, and interpreting our culture and heritage, and increasingly realize its value to the local economy. This mission is too important to the quality of our lives, to our neighborhoods, and to our future, to permit museums to do less than assume a full, active role in their communities.

H. Nicholas Muller, III
Former director, State Historical Society of Wisconsin, Madison, now president and CEO, Frank Lloyd Wright Foundation, Scottsdale, Ariz.

Preface

If this preface acknowledged everyone who contributed to this book, it would become a small catalogue. I need, however, to give special recognition to a few people.

Mark Lane, former director of the Witte Museum, San Antonio, and staff at the Texas Association of Museums (TAM) helped me summon the courage to begin the project. I attended a TAM meeting in 1991, filling out "economic development" as my major interest on the registration form. TAM hosts a reception for newcomers where each new person is matched with a mentor who has similar interests. In my case, the mentor was Mark. He encouraged me to proceed, told me which sessions to attend and whom to contact, spent a day with me when I visited San Antonio a year later, sent me material, returned my phone calls, and provided encouragement. His low-key and courteous manner complement his insightful and ever inquiring mind, realistic "bottom line" thinking, and vision. Many thanks.

In 1990, I called H. Nicholas Muller, III, then director of the State Historical Society of Wisconsin, saying, "You've never heard of me, but would you like to sponsor a project on museums and economic development?" Nick proved an ideal sponsor. His knowledge of the field and contacts within the states of Wisconsin and Washington opened doors. He continued to support the project through numerous grant applications and many delays, and provided expert advice, vision, and good judgment. He also spent time reviewing the manuscript. Both in substance and readability, the manuscript benefited greatly from his attention, for which I am deeply grateful.

All of Nick's staff were courteous, supportive, and friendly. Particular thanks go to Judy Patenaude, Delores "Dee" C. Ducklow, and Eugene Spindler. Judy advised me on the design and printing of a map of museums in northwest Wisconsin, which was part of the overall project. Gene patiently managed the financial aspects of the grant with accuracy and good humor. Besides logistical support, Dee provided common sense, good judgment, and knowledge of Wisconsin, and she was always cheerful. The success of the project owes much to her efforts.

David L. Nicandri, executive director of the Washington State Historical Society, kindly provided support for the project in Washington State. Jerry Dahlke, resource development director, and Michael Warner, director of outreach services, took time from their busy schedules to provide invaluable help, encouragement, and suggestions, and introduced me to the staff at other Washington museums. Steve Anderson, director, Renton Historical Museum, kindly arranged for my presentation to the Washington Museum Association.

Across the nation, museum directors and their staffs generously provided time for interviews in person or by telephone. Particular thanks go to Steve Cotherman, director, Madeline Island Historical Museum; Edgar S. Oerichbauer, executive director of the Burnett County Historical Society and Forts Folle Avoine, Siren, Wis.; and Rachael Martin, executive director of Fairlawn, the headquarters of the Douglas County Historical Society in Superior, Wis.

An *ad hoc* committee provided guidance for development of the collaborative map project. In addition to Rachael, Ed, and Steve, members included Connie Loden, marketing coordinator, Iron County Development Zone Council (who served as chair); Ruth Goetz, tourism development consultant, Wisconsin Department of Tourism; and Lea Justice, then executive director, Chamber of Commerce, Cable, Wis. Nori Newago, president, Image Plus, LaPointe, Wis., served on the committee initially and later coordinated the production of the map. A grant from the International Trade, Business, and Economic Development Council covered the costs of printing, publicizing, and distributing the map.

An advisory committee provided direction, suggestions, and reviewed the manuscript. Thanks go to Robert A. Kret, director, Leigh Yawkey Woodson Museum, and president, Wisconsin Federation of Museums (1995-1997); Steve Cotherman; Ruth Goetz; Pat Hrabik, tribal historic preservation officer/ heritage tourism coordinator, Lac du

Flambeau Band of Lake Superior Chippewa Indians; Stephen Andrews, director, Northwest Regional Planning Commission; and Sharon Folcey, heritage tourism coordinator, Wisconsin Department of Tourism.

Special appreciation goes to Richard E. Hage, former acting director, Research and Technical Assistant Division, Economic Development Administration, U.S. Department of Commerce. He encouraged me to proceed long before the idea of connecting museums to economic development was popular. Thanks also go to Anthony J. Meyer, technical assistant specialist, who monitored the project. Both Dick and Tony exemplify the best meaning of the term public service.

The project would not have been possible without funding provided by the Technical Assistance and Research Division, Economic Development Administration, U.S. Department of Commerce, and sponsorship from the State Historical Society of Wisconsin.

I gathered many of the insights and examples in this book from attendees at numerous meetings on tourism and museums, particularly those organized by the American Association of Museums and the Texas Association of Museums. Speakers graciously shared papers and conversation, and responded to follow-up phone calls. I hope that this book successfully describes the experiences of these skilled and knowledgeable people, as well as the tremendous ways that museums contribute to communities' economic well-being. Final responsibility remains with the author.

Introduction

The word "museums" covers a wide variety of institutions. It includes zoos, art museums, historic houses, college museums, children's museums, science museums, and more. Some museums were developed thorough the efforts of dedicated volunteers. Others employ professional staff, many of whom hold graduate degrees in a variety of subjects.

Most museums, but not all, focus on objects, from paintings and 19th-century costumes to live or mounted animals and dinosaur bones. Traditionally, museums have assumed the responsibility for collecting, preserving, interpreting, exhibiting, and learning about the objects in their collections, and educating all audiences about them. This publication speaks to museum professionals and to public officials, businessmen and others concerned with involving museums in the economic development of their local areas. Clearly what is appropriate for each museum will depend upon its own history, governing board, collection, resources, and other factors.

Museums have always contributed to economic development, a fact that is often overlooked. Recently both museums and economic developers in the United States have become more conscious of their natural partnership. In many places, however, the partnership is not yet formed or the alliance remains uneasy. Too often economic developers ignore the contributions of museums to their efforts, and overlook the potential benefits of closer collaboration.

Sometimes museums operate in a manner that ignores the interests of the local business community. Sometimes they act as though they are above the dirty business of commerce. Yet few museums today can afford to operate solely on endowments or contributions from a few wealthy individuals. Increasingly, they must master intricacies of insurance, discrimination laws, information technologies, and financial forecasting, just like any successful business.

But museums are not simply cultural businesses. To judge museums' value solely by their contribution to local economic development is unrealistic and inappropriate, and will lead to distorted judgments by all involved.

This publication provides both museums and those concerned about economic development with a framework for dialogue. It suggests ways in which closer collaboration can occur, but provides caveats. These examples and suggestions resemble clothing to be tried on for fit. If an idea will not work for your museum or your community, do not use it. None of the ideas can be applied automatically, and none will succeed without considerable discussion between museums and those concerned with economic development.

Either party can begin the dialogue. Addressing the topics in this publication can make the conversations more focused and productive by helping each party to understand the other's perspective and needs, indicating areas of mutual concern, and providing examples of ways museums have made a significant impact on economic development.

1

Demonstrating Museums' Contributions to Economic Development

. . . or What to Tell the Chamber of Commerce

I. Trends Affecting Economic Development

Economic development has various definitions. It can mean the creation of jobs, increase in community or individual income, increase in the taxable base, or increase in wealth for individuals or a community. Planners often consider the following questions: Who benefits and who loses from specific economic development activities? What types of jobs are created and for whom? Building an industrial park with polluting factories damages the ecosystem and reduces the attractiveness of the area for tourists. Consolidating a business operation or replacing workers with a machine may increase wealth for some, but cost the jobs of others.

Trends in economic development rest on responses to changes in the country's economic, social, political and demographic conditions. They also depend upon shifts in the "state of the art" or in the "conventional wisdom" of individuals and institutions who actively work to promote economic growth. These "economic development practitioners" might be chambers of commerce, state departments of development, concerned individual businessmen, political leaders, or other individuals and organizations.

A. The shift from a manufacturing to an information-based economy

Today, people are more likely to spend more time marketing and designing the package for a product than actually making it. Most jobs are no longer located near physical resources such as coal, or man-made infrastructure such as railroad tracks. Many jobs now can be successfully completed in people's homes, with incoming orders received by modem and fax and products delivered by overnight mail.

Implications: Small towns and rural areas are becoming increasingly attractive locations for businesses and for self-employed individuals, especially those who are semi-retired. To the extent that the local museum contributes to an area's general attractiveness, it also contributes to the ability to attract new jobs.

B. The shift to service jobs

More and more people work in service jobs. The service industry now employs more than 75 percent of American workers, a proportion that is expected to continue to increase (Edgell 1993, 4). Contrary to popular opinion, many service jobs pay very well; two examples are lawyers and investment counselors.

Implications: Economic developers sometimes consider tourism jobs unattractive because of their seasonal or low-paying nature. However, many places are now bidding for them. Museums can be a major contributor to the tourism attractiveness of an area. They also offer the type of full-time and volunteer jobs that can develop skills used by better-paid workers in the new service economy: store managers, public relations experts, fundraisers, etc.

C. Small businesses rather than large companies now create the most jobs

In recent years, Fortune 500 companies have not been the main sources of new jobs; many of these companies have reduced their work forces. People starting new businesses or expanding small businesses now create most of the new jobs.

Implications: Many economic development practitioners have stopped trying to lure firms from outside their areas, which too often resulted in unhappy giveaways of tax benefits or community-financed buildings. Instead, they now focus on strategies to help individuals start new businesses and/or expand existing businesses. The money spent by museums locally helps support such efforts. Museums also can help to create spin-off businesses, such as craft shops.

D. Demographic shifts

The American population is aging. The first baby boomers celebrated their 50th birthdays in 1996. Most women, including those with young children, now work outside their homes. Many families have two incomes, but little free time. And the population is increasingly becoming culturally diverse.

Implications: Many older people are looking for places to retire. Others seek second homes, which they can now afford because of their households' double incomes. Those with increased leisure time swell the tourism market. Those with less leisure time seek places for short getaways. Minorities represent an increasing tourism market.

E. Increase in tourism and its economic importance

Tourism—travel for both business and pleasure—is big business. It has become the second-largest employer in the United States; only the health industry employs more people. In 30 states, tourism represents the first-, second- or third-largest employer. Tourism is America's largest export industry (Tourism Works for America Council 1996).

Tourism will continue to grow. The demographics favor it. The potential market in the United State will increase as baby boomers age, have fewer family responsibilities, and eventually retire. Growth in income and education levels, combined with decreased travel time and lower costs of fuel, has led to an increase in pleasure travel, while the growth of an interdependent global economy has increased business travel. In 1995, international tourists spent $79.7 billion in the United States, a 4 percent increase from 1994 (Tourism Works for America Council 1996).

Implications: Museums have much to offer a community's tourism industry. In some small towns, a museum may provide the major reason visitors go to or stop in that area. In 1993, for example, 305,000 people went to Fishers, Ind., to visit Conner Prairie, a historic village. In cities such as New York, museums contribute to a collection of attractions that draw people to the area.

F. Tourism and the potential role for museums

1. Size and importance of tourism for economic development. Tourists spend money. They buy food, tickets, gifts, souvenirs, and lodging. A study of tourist expenditures in Wisconsin found that tourists spent $6.6 billion in 1996 (Davidson-Peterson 1997). Economists count tourism as an export industry because tourists spend money that was made elsewhere. Similar to a manufacturer that exports a product to another state, tourists bring new money into a community.

The money that tourists spend in the community is re-spent by those who receive it. A visitor who purchases a product made in the community increases the income of that business. When the tourist spends money on lodging, the hotel owner may use the money to renovate and paint, and the painter may use that income to buy a television set. The hotel owner, the painter, and the television store have all had increased business—an indirect or *multiplier* effect of spending by tourists. The multiplier effect refers to the number of times a tourist's money is respent on locally produced goods and services within a community.

The impact of this indirect effect of tourist dollars depends upon how much *leakage* occurs. Leakage consists of the portion of the new spending used to purchase goods and services produced outside of the community. In the above example, the painter may have spent part of his fee on paint produced elsewhere. And only a small part of the money used to buy the television set would have stayed within the community, in the form of overhead and profit for the store. The store manager probably sent most of the money to a television wholesaler located outside the area.

Calculating the indirect addition of tourism spending in a community can be either very simple or very complicated, and either quite accurate or very questionable, with experts disagreeing about measurement techniques and accuracy. One approach employs a study that obtains and analyzes records from all the affected businesses over a period of time, and uses sophisticated, computerized models for the calculations. An analysis of the economic impact of nine heritage centers in southwestern Pennsylvania that used this approach concluded that direct sales of $16.8 million resulted in secondary sales of $27 million (Strauss 1994, i).

Another method simply uses a standard multiplier, which typically varies from two to four, again with experts disagreeing about what multiplier to use (Edgell 1993, 20). In some cases, state departments of development will base multipliers for an area upon previous studies.

2. Types of tourism: People travel for many reasons. Economists and the tourist industry place many types of travelers under the category of "tourist," including business travelers and people visiting relatives. People traveling for pleasure do so for a variety of reasons. Some are sports enthusiasts, seeking golf courses, beaches, or hunting grounds. Some haunt museums. Many travel to visit family or friends. Others may seek the excitement of a city or the solitude of an isolated forest.

Recently the tourism industry has begun to actively market heritage tourism, eco-tourism, and cultural tourism, all especially relevant for museums. People like to learn about their roots—the history of their family, community, and nation. They also enjoy learning about the heritage of other groups. Over the past 10 years, the numbers of people saying they are interested in furthering their knowledge of history, culture, or archaeology has grown significantly. In Wisconsin, inquiries to the state's tourism information center about historical tourism jumped from 45,000 in 1990 to 95,000 in 1996.

Eco-tourism describes not something to see but an approach to seeing it. It relates to the concern of environmentalists that tourists should not destroy sensitive natural environments or the culture and social structure of an area's people.

Cultural tourism may include heritage tourism programs as well as musical performances or art exhibits unrelated to the local history. The concepts and use of the terms overlap. For example, *The Cultural Tourism Handbook,* which was produced by Lord Cultural Resources Planning & Management, Inc., Ontario, Canada, defines cultural tourism as "Visits by persons from outside the host community motivated wholly or in part by interest in the historical, artistic, scientific, or lifestyle/heritage offerings of a community, region, group or institution" (Lord 1993, 1). Cultural tourism activities may include: (1) visits to institutions including museums, historic sites, theaters, and performances; (2) visits to heritage districts to learn about ethnic food, other customs, language, or clothing; and (3) events such as festivals, fairs, competitions, and exhibitions.

Conducting a study on tourism for the province of Ontario, Lord found that cultural tourism presents an attractive market for areas concerned with economic development. Tourists interested in culture were more likely to have higher incomes and spend more money than the average tourist, spend time in an area, stay in a hotel or motel rather than with friends or relatives, and more likely to shop (Lord 1993, 3).

The study revealed that 85 percent of the international visitors to Ontario had some interest in cultural attractions. Fifteen percent were greatly motivated by their interest in culture; another 30 percent were partly motivated by Ontario's cultural attractions. Twenty percent said that they might participate in cultural events as a part of a trip taken for another purpose, such as visiting family. Lord identified another 20 percent as "accidental cultural tourists"—people who would not seek out a cultural experience but might attend one if they came across it. Only 15 percent of visitors were unlikely to partake of a cultural event under any circumstances (Lord 1993, 7).

These distinctions have implications for both museums and economic development planners. Both groups would profit by actively marketing to the large segments of potential tourists who are influenced by the availability of cultural attractions when making travel plans. Both groups also could profit by ensuring that visitors in town for other reasons become aware of convenient cultural opportunities within their budgets.

The tourist industry uses the term "destination attraction" to describe a site that serves as the sole or main reason people visit an area. Individual museums rarely serve as destination attractions for the majority of people. However, combined with other attractions, they can be a powerful draw. Sometimes a number of museums will collaborate on a package of related events and programs. When the San Antonio Museum of Art hosted a major exhibit on Mexico, other museums in the city

exhibited Mexican art from their collections and developed related programs. A well-organized publicity campaign promot-
ed all the different events, and more than 131,000 out-of-town
visitors were drawn to the city.

Combining several attractions, which by themselves have limited appeal, into a destination attraction may be particularly important for rural areas and places off the beaten track. Thirty-
eight museums are represented on a map of 12 counties in
northwest Wisconsin. Some of the museums would not be
strong attractions by themselves. Collectively, however, they relate the entire experience of northern Wisconsin's history—
from pre-historic Indian times through the fur trading period
and the later development of the logging, shipping, and mining
industries that supported the growth of the region's cities and
industry.

The authors of *The Cultural Tourism Handbook* suggest that
packaging different types of cultural attractions—for example,
a museum and a concert—may appeal to a broader audience.
Even more effective packaging may pair non-cultural attractions—such as sports events and shopping malls—with cultural
ones. Tourists who are not highly motivated to visit an area
solely to see a museum may be attracted by a package that
gives them something to do on a rainy day or in the evening.

Tourism is only one way that museums can contribute to economic development. Museums fit into the larger economic development picture in several other ways.

II. Demonstrating Museums' Economic Contributions

A. Museums spend money

Nationally, museums have become a $4.4-billion industry. To-
gether, they spend more money than many state governments

(Grogg 1994, 83). Every time a museum pays its employees or buys supplies locally, it helps the local economy. If a museum attracts visitors from another state to the area, and they buy lunch or shop, that brings new money into the community. When a museum spends money obtained from outside the area, it is acting as an "export industry," similar to a local manufacturer that sends products to other states or nations.

1. Sources of outside money
(a) *Federal and state money*: The federal government directly funds the Smithsonian Institution and museums operated by the National Park Service and the Department of Defense, among others. Their expenditures benefit the nearby communities. The federal government also provides funds directly and indirectly to museums throughout the country through programs in such diverse agencies as the Departments of Education and Transportation, the National Endowments for the Arts and Humanties, and the Institute of Museum and Library Services. Total federal government support for museums has been declining and competition for state funds is increasing. Nevertheless, both remain major contributors to museums, providing 14 percent of total museum budgets (American Association of Museums 1996, 3).

(b) *Foundations and corporations:* Foundations and corporations contribute to museums. Non-local support for special exhibits or other purposes brings outside money to a community. Sometimes they are local organizations, but their contributions and endowment income may come from non-local sources, such as former residents.

(c) *Endowments:* Money from endowments comes from investments, generally in businesses or financial instruments outside the community. This income flows back into the museum's community. The number of museums with endowments jumped almost 20 percent between 1989 and 1996. The value of these endowments grew even more markedly, from a median value of $125,000 in 1989 to $750,000 in 1996. By 1996, the majority of museums had endowments. Of the museums with membership in the American Association of Museums, the numbers ranged from 55 percent for small museums to almost 75 percent for mid-sized ones to almost 90 percent for large museums (American Association of Museums 1996, 18).

(d) *Trustees or members who live elsewhere:* Another source of outside income comes from people who formerly lived in or are regular visitors to the area. One town of 800 in Wisconsin has a number of summer cottages owned by people from Minneapolis, Chicago, Milwaukee, and Racine. The local museum has cultivated a core of eight to 10 loyal trustees who live in these cities. Jointly, they contribute approximately $60,000 to the museum budget every year. The museum, in turn, spends these funds locally.

The Madeline Island Historical Museum, LaPointe, Wis., located on one of the Apostle Islands in the northern part of the state, also benefits from part-time residents. The year-round population is 187. But in the summer, it swells to 3,000, including seasonal homeowners and tourists. The museum's director considers himself lucky. The museum has "a patron network that's been built up from the '50s. The friends and family of the founders have a feeling of ownership in the museum," he says. "A number of the same people give $100 or $200 every fall. It's an old museum tradition. We're now dealing with their kids, who give . . . in memory of their parents and grandparents. It's a generational tradition."

(e) *Sales to visitors from outside the area:* Museums do earn money. In 1988, the museum community earned $1.1 billion. This figure includes revenue generated from admissions, memberships, gift shops, restaurants, parking, and publications, as well as services to other museums (Grogg 1994, 89). By 1996, earned income had become the leading source of funds for museums, accounting for one-third of their total operating income (American Association of Museums 1996, ii). Income from gift shops and publications ranged from a median of $15,000 to a high of $19 million, with the average just under $200,000. When visitors purchasing these admissions and gifts come from outside the local community, they help make the museum a part of the community's export industry.

(f) *Sales of museum products or services outside the area:* The director of the Forts Folle Avoine, a historic site and museum in Siren, Wis., is an archaeologist. Each year, he and his staff conduct archaeological surveys, which are required for builders using federal funds. The 15 to 30 projects that his team conducts annually net between $95,000 and $225,000, money that the museum spends locally.

B. Museums provide jobs
Types of jobs typically found in a museum:
1. director and management staff
2. curators and other professionals who care for and interpret the collection
3. educational directors, guides, interpreters
4. security personnel
5. maintenance and janitorial staff
6. ticket takers
7. shop manager
8. shop clerks
9. exhibit designers and builders
10. volunteer coordinator
11. membership developers, marketing directors, and fundraisers

C. Museums support local businesses
1. *Examples of goods purchased locally*

a. material for building expansion, renovation, or exhibit
   construction
b. paint
c. office supplies
d. art supplies
e. film and development
f. food
g. crafts for the shop
h. materials for costumes
i. computers and other office equipment
j. furniture

2. Examples of services purchased locally
a. carpentry
b. brick masonry
c. telephone and other utilities
d. bookkeeping
e. catering
f. photography
g. computer maintenance and consultation
h. artistic design
i. management of endowment funds or investment advice

D. Museums enhance the quality of life, community pride, and public education

Museums can help create an ambience for a town through exhibits, special events, and outreach to schools and other organizations. By displaying and celebrating a community's heritage, a museum can acknowledge the importance and validity
of local residents' contributions and lives. Many museums host
numerous school visits, which often function as an important
part of the school system's curriculum.

These contributions make the town or region a more desirable
area. They also assist economic development by attracting sec-
ond-home owners and retired residents, encouraging new busi-

nesses to locate in the area, and helping current businesses remain in the community. Museums also can play a role with local employers recruiting new managers. From Amarillo, Tex., to Wausau, Wis., employers take prospective management candidates to museums "to let them know they are not being dropped into a cultural wasteland," says one director.

E. Museums attract tourists

Everyone knows that people take their children to Washington, D.C., to see the National Air and Space Museum, the National Gallery of Art, and the dinosaurs in the National Museum of Natural History. Who would have thought that 131,000 people would go to San Antonio to see "Mexico: Splendors of Thirty Centuries"? But they did. Local people came, too, making total attendance 265,000. Visitors to the exhibition spent $80 million. Compare that figure to the $2.5-million exhibition cost.

Who gained from the $80 million? Retail stores—$15 million; restaurants—$27 million; hotels—$40 million; the state government (through hotel/motel and sales taxes)—$5 million; and the San Antonio city government—$2.8 million in hotel and transit taxes. The city's share almost equaled the cost of its annual budget for all arts programs.

Smaller museums may not have collections that could serve as a destination attraction for thousands of people. Nevertheless, a small museum may contribute to tourism development in four ways:

1. A museum can contribute to the overall ambience of the town, thus making it a more interesting or pleasant place to visit . . . and to live.

2. A museum can join with museums in nearby towns to create an attractiveregional package.

Many towns are like Fall River, Mass., in that they can claim a few attractions, but are not destinations. Fall River, the home

of Lizzie Borden and the site of several museums, is off the
beaten track. But instead of competing with neighboring
towns, Fall River joined with them. They created the Ameri-
cana Trail, a recreational and vacation guide to coastal New
England. During its first four years, this collective effort
brought $2.5 million into Bristol County (Weaver 1986, 143).

3. A museum can sponsor, or help sponsor, special events that
turn an area into a destination site, even if only for a day or
weekend.

Forts Folle Avoine focuses on the history of the Ojibwe Indians
and the fur trade. Each July, the museum sponsors an annual
Forts Folle Avoine Rendezvous Weekend. More than 300 people, dressed as fur traders and American Indians, camp on the
museum grounds or stay in local hotels. The normal number of
summer weekend tourists to the museum is about 500. But
during the Rendezvous Weekend, the total ranges from 2,600
to 3,000. The economic impact for the community is between
$125,000 and $175,000, depending upon the method of calcu-
lation used.

4. Visiting a museum can increase the amount of time a tourist
stays in the community. The longer visitors stay in an area, the
more money they spend. The longer they linger at attractions,
the more likely they are to remain in town to have lunch or
dinner or even to spend the night.

According to Marion Munson, owner of the Time Out Restaurant in Washburn, Wis., the new local museum helps her business. "It's a total asset, which has brought more people downtown," she says. "They go over to the museum and ask where's
a good place to eat. . . . They come to the activities at the museum and they stay the weekend. They say, 'as long as we're going to the museum at 7:00 [for an event], why don't we go
downtown early, do some shopping and have a bite to eat, then
go over to the museum?'"

Thus, museums can contribute to economic development of any community. In many cases, they could make even larger contributions by consciously planning their efforts and working cooperatively with local business people and officials concerned with economic development.

References

AAM 1996 Museum Financial Information Survey. Washington, D.C.: American Association of Museums, 1996.

Davidson-Peterson Associates, Inc. *The Economic Impact of Expenditures by Travelers on Wisconsin.* York, Maine: Davidson-Peterson Associates, Inc., 1997.

Edgell, David L., Sr. *World Tourism at the Millennium.* Washington, D.C.: U.S. Department of Commerce, U.S. Travel and Tourism Administration, 1993.

Grogg, Ann Hofstra. Project Writer and Editor. *Museums Count.* Washington, D.C.: American Association of Museums, 1994.

Lord Cultural Resources Planning & Management Inc. *The Cultural Tourism Handbook.* Ontario, Canada: Lord Cultural Resources Planning & Management Inc., 1993.

Marano, Helen. *International Travel Trends.* Washington, D.C.: U.S. Travel and Tourism Administration, 1995.

Strauss, Charles H. *Economic Impacts and User Expenditures from Selected Heritage Visitor Centers: 1993. Part I.* Hollidaysburg, Penn.: Southwestern Pennsylvania Heritage Preservation Commission, 1994.

Tourism Works for America 1996 Report. Washington, D.C.: Tourism Works for America Council, 1996.

U.S. Travel Data Center. *A Portrait of Travel Industry Employment in the U.S. Economy.* Washington, D.C.: Travel Industry Association of America Foundation, 1994.

Weaver, Glenn. *Tourism USA: Guidelines for Tourism Development.* Columbia, Mo.: The University of Missouri, 1986.

2

Potential Advantages
for Museums

Any museum considering becoming more involved in economic development will want to consider carefully the benefits and costs, as well as the most appropriate ways to participate. Economic development practitioners desiring to maximize the benefits of their town's museum should be aware of its institutional concerns and limitations, as well as the potential advantages of collaboration.

I. What Is the Museum's Role? Know Thyself

A. The collection
What does the museum have to offer? Who will want to see the collection? How many and what kinds of people will the collection attract? Does it include items such as illuminated medieval manuscripts or fading photographs that would limit display possibilities or restrict the number of viewers? What balance between protecting and sharing its collection does the museum desire or accept?

B. The mission

What is the museum's mission? Are certain activities, such as research, stressed more than others, such as education? Is the mission to educate the largest number of children about the concepts of science or to preserve a small town's objects of historical interest? The director of one historical society on the West Coast says, a major part of his mission is to preserve and index local newspapers, thus making them accessible to historians. But, though both time-consuming and expensive, that aspect of his museum's mission will not attract many visitors.

Some museums' missions dovetail with economic development more comfortably than others. Some museums have added economic development to their mission statements. For other museums, that may be undesirable or unrealistic.

C. The audience

Who is the existing audience? If the museum leadership does not understand the current audience, how will they expand it or add new audiences? How many visitors does the museum want? Whom does the museum want to attract? What kind of an experience should they have? How long should they stay? From where do they come, and where does increased market potential exist? How much will this audience pay for admission or spend in the store? The answers to these questions relate clearly to questions of mission, collection, and personnel.

The more carefully a museum's leaders think through these issues, the more likely it is that they will select economic development activities consistent with the institution's mission and operations. One director gave a heated response to the notion that the tourism market for Wisconsin's museums should target higher-income, professional, well-educated people, those more likely to be found drinking wine at an upscale hotel than drinking beer at a camp site. He said that those people already knew about museums; his mission was to expand the interests of less-educated people. That is a legitimate concern. But if this director's mission is used as a basis for allocating marketing resources, it will not provide as much revenue as resources targeted to the museum's most favorable tourism market.

D. Finances

Recently, the interest in the connection between museums and economic development has increased dramatically. One reason is the current climate of budget reductions at all levels of government; another is the rising costs for many basic museum operations.

Does the museum depend on the support of local government? Many historical museums in the state of Washington, for example, are county institutions. While there was a constant stream of support in the past, this may no longer be secure. Does the museum expect to lose substantial support from federal grants? Is competition with foundations growing because of the increase in the number of museums, cuts in government funding for social programs, and a general movement away from funding operating expenses? Does the museum need more staff because the pool of volunteers, traditionally female, has eroded as older women pass on and younger women now work or attend college full-time?

The answers to these questions will help determine the benefits to an institution participating in local economic development efforts. If a museum needs good will from local city council representatives, hosting an annual event honoring important events or persons in the town's history may prove more useful than sponsoring an exhibit of rare European prints. But if the local government is anxious to attract tourists, the opposite may be the case.

E. Trustees, staff, and volunteers

If you do not include trustees, staff, and volunteers in economic development planning, you are asking for trouble. Remember that a museum's very limited resources include staff time.
And staff members often perceive new activities as taking attention from existing projects or priorities. Economic development activities may demand different actions or attitudes from
them. A historical museum serving as a community center that
provides morning coffee for older volunteers will have a different atmosphere if it begins attracting bus tours of people who
must be attended to promptly and efficiently. Such shifts can
create resistance and disagreements, which are best addressed
candidly up-front. At the very least, trustees, staff, and volunteers should agree that it is appropriate for museum resources
and time to be spent on economic development activities.

However, undertaking economic development activities can
give existing trustees, staff, and volunteers countless opportunities to share and develop new skills and contacts and to further their own desire to help the museum. They also may have
contacts and knowledge in economic development, publicity,
marketing, managing shops, or sponsoring festivals.

II. Advantages to Increased Participation

A. More visitors

Museums house collections with treasures that can fascinate
people. Some have outstanding examples of world-famous
masters, such as the paintings by El Greco in the Toledo Art
Museum, Ohio. Even without such treasures, a museum's collections properly exhibited will help people understand themselves and their culture. The exhibits at Forts Folle Avoine, a
reconstructed fort and museum in Siren, Wis., stress the mutual advantages of the contacts between the fur traders and the

Indians, and the history of their interaction starting in the
1600s.

Few museums have so many visitors that they do not want
more. Even museums that experience occasional crowding may
want larger audiences at certain times of the year or a wider
cross-section of people.

B. Increased revenue

More visitors means increased revenue through more admission fees, food purchases, and shop purchases. New visitors
become prospects for recruitment as members, participants at
seminars or festivals, donors, and funders.

Rising visitor numbers will impress local governments and
businesses, and make them more receptive to increasing financial and other support. Trustees and foundations want to know
"how many people you serve." In an era of budget cut-backs,
continued federal, state, and local support for museums will
depend upon whether a large number of people believe that
museums make a significant contribution to the community.

C. Ability to fulfill educational mission

If more people come, more people will learn. Attempting to
expand their audiences, museums may provide many learning
opportunities—from text labels to formal programs. If the museum's programs and exhibits are designed to provide successful learning experiences for individuals with different interests
and learning styles, the educational mission is more likely to be
fulfilled. If increased attendance results in more funding, either
directly or indirectly, that may create additional resources for
educational exhibits.

D. Ability to fulfill research and curatorial missions

The greater the number and variety of people who appreciate a
museum, the more likely funds for fulfilling other goals will be-

come available. This particularly applies if the exhibits themselves can display some of the curatorial and research functions. The Logan Museum of Anthropology at Beloit College,
Beloit, Wis., renovated the museum with the visitor in mind.
The director "brought upstairs what used to be downstairs,"
and turned the storage and work space into an exhibit. Glass
walls permit the visitor to see the rows of Indian pottery on the
shelves and watch the students and curators as they catalog
and care for the objects.

E. Collection development

People who visit museums sometimes have items or even entire
collections to donate.

F. More respect and support from the community

By participating more actively and visibly in a community's
economic development efforts, a museum positions itself to be
recognized as an important partner in the community's life and
future, rather than simply a nice place for an occasional visit.

III. Things to Consider

A. Losing sight of collection responsibilities

Museums have multiple roles, but they typically revolve around
collections—collecting, preserving, and interpreting. Collections take staff time and attention, and require money. Visitors
and funders often do not understand the cost of managing collections beyond those they see on exhibit. Preservation often
requires expensive environmental controls and hours of
painstaking labor. Museums will need to show their collections
management efforts to outsiders, and explain the importance
of funds for these activities. This will help create understanding of the museum's need to set realistic limits on its other activities.

B. Museums are not theme parks

The mission of any museum goes far beyond entertainment. Most museums would agree that enjoying the museum experience enhances visitor learning. But if taken too far, the desire to "sell the product" can dilute the exhibits' historical accuracy and artistic integrity.

Carefully employed, however, entertainment techniques can further a museum's educational mission by making the museum user-friendly. A famous and successful restaurant owner in Chicago claimed that he served flaming steaks because "it pleases the customers and it doesn't hurt the food." The museum is not a restaurant, but an institution of trust. Museum traditions call for accurate scholarship and intellectual honesty, even when treating controversial subjects. Nevertheless, a message based on good research and intellectual integrity can be enhanced using modern technology and a variety of delivery methods, in a manner that does not change its content.

C. Museums are not Wall Street

Making money is not a museum's main mission. If a museum neglects curatorial tasks to take on more and more money-making projects, it eventually could find that it has nothing left to display. One museum professional says that if he shifted his budget to provide more programs, "my collections would suffer, my educational role would suffer, my research would suffer. In the long run, I'd suck the heart out of [my museum], and pretty soon I'd be marketing a shell."

A balance is necessary. The correct balance will differ for each museum. A historic home, for example, should take into account the wear and tear on the building. "The house itself is an antique and [in] everything we do here, even the cleaning products [we use], we have to regard our environment as an antique," says Rachael Martin, director of the Fairlawn Mansion and Museum, Superior, Wis.

Martin's trustees "see the museum the same way everyone in the community sees the museum, the programs, [and] the visible aspects." But they quickly become "enlightened" about the "nuts and bolts" when she provides behind-the-scenes tours. Martin also constantly undertakes more subtle education projects, such as distributing short articles dealing with aspects addressed by trustee committees. One of her more successful strategies has been to hold trustee meetings in various rooms in the museum. As they sit in a meeting for several hours, the trustees "gawk around a bit," gradually gaining a more intimate appreciation of the room. Trustees will comment, "Oh, look at all the work going on in this room. I didn't notice the floors were in such bad shape. That's a good way to fix them." To provide trustees with additional confidence in her recommendations for preservation work, Martin sometimes invites an expert widely respected in the community, such as an architect, to committee meetings.

D. Shifts in direction require support from trustees, staff, and volunteers

Trustees, especially those of small museums, sometimes donate important parts of collections and want them displayed "just like when grandma had it." Volunteers who have been handling major responsibilities may feel that exhibit displays are "their turf." A number of museums are adopting business practices, such as strategic planning, to examine how their institutions function, consider changes, and build new agreements among all participants.

In 1986, the Outagamie County Historical Society, Appleton, Wis., adopted a five-year plan, which was revised in 1992. Since the adoption of the first plan, the society has completed restoration of both the Outagamie Museum and the Charles A. Grignon Mansion, an 1837 Greek Revival home; opened a prize-winning exhibit, "Tools of Change"; and mounted an exhibit about Houdini. The society also raised $5.6 million, half of which was used for an endowment that supports four positions.

Then-Director Donald R. Hoke said that the strategic plan was crucial to achieving these successes: The plan represents "decisions about what you want to get accomplished. . . . [It] defines what you do when you [go to work] in the morning and [helps to] allocate scarce resources."

Creating such plans forces trustees and board members to focus, make decisions, and consciously affirm values and approaches. Often, the basic mission declared in the articles of incorporation has not been re-examined in years. Frequently, even trustees who use business techniques in their own operations must be helped to realize that museums need to employ the same techniques.

Strategic plans also reduce confusion and potential conflict, particularly for new staff and volunteers. They also clarify what a particular museum is *not*. This enables staff to respond to an enthusiastic board member with a pet project or a volunteer with a gift of an unneeded artifact by asking them how it relates to the strategic plan.

E. Do not overwork the collection

Some objects, such as rare Japanese prints, should not be exposed to light on a constant basis, as ultraviolet waves will fade the colors. The Elvehjem Museum of Art in Madison, Wis., responded to this problem by having temporary exhibitions at regular intervals that displayed different prints from the museum's extensive collection of Japanese works.

Many smaller historical museums have such limited funds that their objects, especially photographs and negatives, are rapidly deteriorating due to lack of proper care. Occasional displays of selected objects, or photographs of them, that include an explanation of conservation needs and techniques might actually contribute to preservation by stimulating interest and funds.

F. Security problems

Security problems are real whether you have one new volunteer or thousands of visitors. Increasing the number and complexity of exhibits and events, as well as the number of staff and visitors, increases a museum's risks. Museums have suffered theft of objects and store merchandise by staff, volunteers, researchers, students, and visitors. Carefully checking people's credentials and references, and good supervision and detailed planning of traffic flow, exhibit design, and admission control can alleviate problems. Other directors, especially those with similarly sized museums and similar types of collections, can provide suggestions. The American Association of Museums has publications on security and many standard works on museum management that include information on security (see the bibliography).

G. Loss in quality of experience because of crowds

An extensive study of visitor reactions to 11 major art museums found that people experienced exhilaration, awe, and excitement. One visitor described a work as "the most breathtaking piece of art I have ever seen in my life. I just sat there and looked and looked and looked. It was totally incredible. . . . I got chilled; that isn't even the word for it" (Walsh 1991, 14).

Such an in-depth experience becomes difficult when someone else's head is between the visitor and the painting. Crowding can present a serious problem, especially for art museums. It helps to post labels at a distance from the picture. Another solution is to route traffic flow far enough away from the works so that they can be seen from a proper viewing distance and by more than one person at a time. Museums are not always successful in this effort. The organizers of a major exhibit of Im-

pressionist works placed a guide string on the floor about 1
foot in front of the paintings. Although the string prevented
people from moving closer, it also encouraged them to walk exactly 1 foot in front of the painting—which neither provided
good viewing positions for the large Impressionist works nor
permitted viewing by more than one visitor at once. An exhibit
of Japanese screens had security devices that beeped every time
a viewer came within several feet of the objects. The noise from
the beeps destroyed the atmosphere of quiet contemplation
evoked by the works of art.

The location of audio-tour outlets also influences how many
people can appreciate the picture at the same time and
whether anyone can see the entire painting without a head in
the way. Marketing the museum's other exhibits and activities,
such as slide shows occurring outside the exhibit area, can help
even out visitor flow. Many museums also limit the number of
people permitted in an exhibit at one time.

H. Financial loss

Not all economic development activities prove financially successful (see chapter 6 for more on this topic). Before participating in a venture, those responsible for economic development
should analyze the project and clarify expectations with everyone involved. Planners also should keep good records and conduct a dispassionate follow-up evaluation to determine which
activities to undertake a second time.

I. Overselling museums' economic development contributions

The major roles of museums are collection, preservation, research, and education, whether or not they benefit the local
economy. Overselling economic development can become a
very serious problem. Not all museums can become major
tourist attractions. Even those that do probably will not contribute as much to the local economy as some other types of
enterprises.

If the museum oversells its potential economic contribution, it runs the risk of losing support to other enterprises that can prove that their efforts will create more local jobs and wealth. Museums' economic development contributions, however, can provide an argument for financial support. If, after carefully weighing the pros and cons, a museum director decides that promoting the museum's role in local economic development would be a benefit, a number of options exist.

IV. Structuring Participation

Having determined its level of involvement in economic development, a museum can then work out how best to proceed. In most cases, the community will have many individuals and organizations already involved in economic development or related activities. Key players often include chambers of commerce, local units of government, economic development planning districts or organizations, downtown revitalization committees, planning departments or staffs of local colleges or universities, Agricultural Extension Service staff, banks, owners or directors of major businesses, and service clubs such as the Rotary.

Before starting, identify the major existing players and find out how they operate. Members of the board, staff, and volunteers can serve as good sources of information. In some cases, the director and a board member may approach an organization together. In many communities, the players in economic development are numerous, overlapping, and sometimes competitive. Wisdom dictates proceeding cautiously and learning as much as possible before jumping in. This approach allows you to identify how the museum can make its best contribution within the framework of its own goals.

Contact other area museums and providers of cultural services and explore forming cooperative alliances (examples of regional cooperation will be considered in chapter 5). When making these contacts, think broadly. Talk to the owners of art-related businesses such as galleries and antique dealers. Plan participation so that local businesses and others do not perceive your efforts as unwelcome competition.

After learning what economic development efforts are in the works, the museum's leadership can re-think its potential contributions more realistically. Should the museum become an active member of an existing team? Can the museum supply new leadership? Or will its best choice be to remain an outsider or play on the margin?

Chapter 3 will consider ways to make a museum more attractive to tourists and develop partnerships with others in economic development-related activities. Remember that museums may have some hidden assets. In many smaller communities, the museum's director, staff, board members, and volunteers are among the most educated persons in the community. They may have planning and organizational skills of particular value to an economic development effort. They may have seen the latest methods in strategic planning, evaluation, and computer technology at national conferences, or may have read about economic development efforts in professional journals.

Museums often command respect similar to that granted religious institutions and universities. Museum directors may be considered sources of objectivity and neutral analysis. If various community fractions are arguing, merely hosting the meeting in the museum may provide a neutral "turf" and help resolve issues. Of course, not all museums or their personnel will command this type of respect.

Museums often have staff with expertise on local history and on the diverse heritage of the region, who can provide insights and perspective to community discussions. Recently, many museums have started highlighting the contributions that native peoples and other minority groups have made to their local areas. For years, the Red River Historical Museum, Sherman, Tex., represented only the culture of the community's Caucasian residents. An outreach effort to the public, libraries, and older members of the African-American community, combined with research into the museum's own collection, resulted in an exhibit called "The Black History of Grayson County," which opened with a record crowd (Hooper 1995, 8). The Texas Association of Museums has developed an excellent publication, *Action Plan: Multicultural Initiatives in Texas Museums,* which provides detailed and extraordinarily insightful and sensitive suggestions to museums concerned with their roles in multicultural leadership (Hooper 1995).

In 1994, the Mint Museum of Art, Charlotte, N.C., united 25 organizations in a collaborative effort to educate the public about HIV/AIDS. They created a museum exhibit consisting of life masks and oral histories. "Project Face to Face" attracted 17,927 visitors and reached many more through extensive media coverage and programs developed by the collaborating organizations. All of the many letters to the local paper about the exhibit were positive. And one young visitor wrote in the gallery comment book, "I leave this place greatly changed. This exhibit . . . allowed me to actually realize how AIDS affects everyone."

As it becomes a more active economic development player, a museum will need to consider its role carefully to avoid becoming a target of community resentment. Often, the respect granted museums as places of knowledge is mixed with contempt for their staffs, who are seen as "ivory tower," non-practical people who know nothing about reality or business. One way for museums to overcome this is by learning business terms, approaching projects in a business-like manner, and articulating the museum's business contributions. The next chap-

ter will consider ways in which museums can make themselves
more attractive to tourists, thus participating more fully in economic development activities. Approaching economic development in a business-like manner is the wisest way for a museum
to use its limited resources.

References

Hooper, Gena Kwon, ed. *Action Plan: Multicultural Initiatives in
Texas Museums.* Austin, Tex.: Texas Association of Museums, 1995.

Walsh, Amy, ed. *Insights: Museums Visitors Attitudes Expectations: A
Focus Group Experiment.* Los Angeles: The J. Paul Getty Trust, 1991.

Product Development: Increasing Attractiveness to Tourists

From the point of view of economic development, a museum is a product—something that attracts visitors. Like any business manager, a museum director must consider how well the product will sell. The director must make sure that people interested in the product know about it and find it easily accessible.

This chapter suggests 12 ways a museum can make itself more attractive and available to visitors. The suggestions have evolved from interviews with museum directors and economic development professionals in the states of Washington and Wisconsin; attendees at national and regional conferences on museums, economic development, and tourism; as well as from my observations at more than 300 museums in over 30 countries.

I. Visitor Services

Visitor service starts before anyone enters the museum, and involves several considerations. Is the museum well advertised with clear directions for car and bus access? Are there posted signs with entrances and parking lots clearly noted? Are the parking facilities available, convenient, and well lit? When visitors enter the museum, will they feel welcomed or overwhelmed? Are staff and volunteers accessible, friendly, and knowledgeable? Are restrooms and food areas clearly identified, clean, and pleasant? Could a visitor to a large facility leave after an hour without seeing the most important holdings, simply because she did not know the museum displayed them?

II. Attractive Exhibits

Economic development professionals often are frustrated by their local museum's exhibits. Visitors, one complained, are not attracted by a stuffed bird "dead on the table."

What makes an exhibit attractive to tourists? In recent years, the museum profession has transformed its exhibit approaches and technologies (see the bibliography for more information on this topic). As Robert Kret, director of the Leigh Yawkey Museum, Wausau, Wis., observes, museum exhibit philosophy has also changed. The traditional approach made the visitor dependent on guided tours or labels provided by experts for all information. Today, audio-taped guides, interactive exhibits and videos, and computer information stations enable visitors to set their own pace. Kret suggests that future approaches will create interdependence among visiting families as museums begin to develop multi-generational activities and gallery discussions. While some of these new exhibit principles are time consuming and expensive, many of them can be adapted by museums with small budgets. A small museum with one professional staff member may have outstanding exhibits, while a larger museum may display a major collection so badly that it is difficult to see or appreciate the objects.

The High Desert Museum, Bend, Oreg., has developed excellent approaches that can serve as models for almost every museum. The museum contains a series of interconnected dioramas portraying life in the High Desert at different times in history; a gift shop with relevant items; paintings and sculpture that depict the desert and its inhabitants; live animals, including otters and porcupines; an amphitheater for live bird-of-prey presentations; outdoor exhibits of trees common to the area as well as the machinery used to log them; a pioneer wagon and homestead; a wildlife observation area; and an indoor/outdoor exhibit pavilion on managing the ponderosa pine ecosystem.

The museum benefited enormously from the work of a former director who developed a compelling vision and raised considerable funds to implement it. Many of these elements could be adopted, perhaps on a smaller scale and with less expense. Some possibilities include:

A. Paying attention to the unique features of the region's ecology

The Cable Natural History Museum, in the small town of Cable, Wis., emphasizes the ecology of its area. Unlike the High Desert Museum, it does not have a multi-acre site. But the museum has developed a self-guided five-mile walking tour on land 10 miles away that is owned by one of its supporters. The tour's guidebook identifies and discusses many concepts also exhibited in the museum. The director estimates that 1,000 to 1,500 people walk the nature trail each year.

B. Exhibiting works by local artists that illustrate the region's natural or human environment

The director of the High Desert Museum identified appropriate works of art and then asked wealthy individuals to purchase them for the museum. While not all museums can afford expensive collections of bronze sculpture or oil paintings, many might be able to find benefactors willing to purchase less expensive forms of art, such as photographs. Or they could emulate the Ilwaco Heritage Museum, Ilwaco, Wash., which annually hosts a show of the region's artists.

An additional advantage to incorporating art into any museum is that it appeals to visitors who are not interested in historic or technological exhibits. Encouraged by several people, I visited the excellent Maritime Museum in Astoria, Wash. Though I had very little interest in ships or naval technology, I found the museum's marvelous paintings and photographs of ships entrancing.

C. Displaying live animals

Not every museum can afford an otter pool. But some could manage a small aquarium or terrarium. A museum may not want to encage birds, but it could place bird feeders outside a window. Any museum considering this approach needs to research applicable laws and regulations, and select animals that can be cared for and exhibited without harm, given its facilities and staff schedules.

D. Reflecting the museum's mission in the gift shop

Although many museum stores sell items unrelated to their specific mission (paying the appropriate federal "unrelated business income tax"), many also report that their best-selling items are books that expand upon their exhibit themes. Edgar Oerichbauer, director of Forts Folle Avoine, an Ojibwe village and reconstructed fur trading post in Siren, Wis., advocates a close relationship between the museum's store and its mission and holdings. He "set up and stocked [the store using] the same philosophy as our visitation experience," stressing quality and authenticity, he says. The store sells crafts handmade by members of the local Ojibwe tribe. This approach has proven successful; the store grossed $50,000 last year, which compares favorably with stores in similar museums. "You have to pay the price to start with," says Oerichbauer. "If you get into a tourism market your net profits are higher in the near term, but soon your store has a reputation of being merely another tourist shop." The store now draws repeat customers looking for special gifts for weddings and holidays. Recently, Oerich-bauer talked with someone who had driven 120 miles from Eau Claire, Wis., simply to shop. (For a detailed discussion of this issue, see the introduction and pages 186-189 in *Museum Store Management* by Mary Miley Theobald.)

E. Remembering silence
The audio for the first diorama at the High Desert Museum consists of quiet sounds similar to those that might be heard at a marsh in the early morning: the songs of birds and gentle winds rustling in the grass and trees. The sound effects provide the visitor with an enhanced awareness of life in the desert.

Any exhibit intended to inspire a sense of awe needs to provide visitors with space, time, and some degree of solitude. This seems, at first, to counter the emphasis on attracting more people. Sometimes museums limit the number of people who can enter an exhibit at a time, but good exhibit design and space management also can help to accommodate the audience while creating a feeling of solitude. Self-directed audio tours are quieter than docents. The National Gallery, London, placed a rare Leonardo da Vinci drawing in a circular enclosure with limited seating and dim lights. This design encouraged quiet contemplation.

F. Using storage to advantage
The High Desert Museum's collection includes valuable leather-bound books. The director enclosed an area approximately 10 feet by 3 feet, and set up a 19th-century gentleman's library. This transformed shelves of stored books into an interesting exhibit.

G. Making it interactive

Interactivity can be accomplished with low technology approaches. The High Desert Museum's outdoor area has seeds displayed in plastic cases with signs asking visitors to identify them. Visitors lift a piece of wood to discover the answers, which are hidden underneath. Interactive exhibits can be especially important in appealing to people who learn best from experience rather than from reading or lectures.

H. Having something for people with different interests

The High Desert Museum appeals to those who like history, animals, technology, the natural environment, or art. Similarly, the Whyte Museum of the Canadian Rockies, Banff, Canada, uses approaches that can be easily adopted by almost any historical society. I had not planned to visit Banff's museums, but became ill during a ski holiday and wandered into one. The Whyte Museum features the history of Banff and, in one exhibit, the history of tourism in Banff. I was not inclined to learn about the city's history and even less interested in its tourism experience. But the museum had recreated the turn-of-the-century lobby of a famous local hotel, complete with registration desk, fashionably dressed lady, trunk with foreign travel stickers, and a child playing with a doll. More important, the people portrayed represented a real family that vacationed in Banff regularly. The exhibit included photographs of the family and letters they had written to friends. I found myself with my nose pressed against the glass for 20 minutes despite my initial lack of interest.

Other exhibits in the museum also used historical figures to enliven history. In one, a mannequin dressed as a trail guide stood surrounded by guns and other equipment, each with a label explaining the necessity of the particular piece. Behind the mannequin, photographs and text told the life story of a real Banff trail guide. Other mannequins portrayed the area's Native Americans, climbers, photographers, and railroad builders. None of the exhibit areas were large; one was tucked into a corner of the room. Together, however, the 19 figures provided a vivid and captivating portrait of the history of the town.

These small exhibits used elements that most museums could employ:
1. real people as examples
2. photographs
3. letters

Other museums using a similar philosophy have employed:
1. quotations from people who remember the individual
2. real people on tape or video
3. docents who personally remember "how it used to be"

When asked a question about an exhibit on fish seining, a volunteer at the Ilwaco Heritage Museum, Ilwaco, Wash., responded briefly, and then related a Tom Sawyer-type adventure from his childhood: He and some buddies stole a boat and lived on an island, where they camped for a week until a fisherman told them their families thought they were dead. This gave the visitors a memorable example of the atmosphere of the town 40 years earlier and made the exhibits more interesting and effective.

Arminta Neal, a museum exhibits expert, suggests that museums select and organize objects "into a meaningful story," created either by tracing the history of an object, area, or people, or by showing a comparison among related objects (Neal 1987, 5). The Wisconsin Veterans Museum, Madison, has dioramas that represent six wars. Each one contains seven themes: weapons used, medicine and food, soldiers' leisure-time activities, strategy and tactics, clothing, and the roles of women and minorities. This approach provides depth to each exhibit as well as a historical perspective of the changes in these factors over time.

Neal suggests that the first job of a local historical museum is to tell the local story in depth. Her questions for museums include: Why is the town where it is? Who came here first? Who were the first non-Indian settlers? Why does the town still exist (Neal 1987, 8)?

Since most people spend "no more than 30 to 45 seconds viewing a single display," a museum must focus its attention on the key parts of the story (Neal 1987, 22). The Panhandle Plains Historical Museum, Canyon, Tex., has a collection of old and colorful Texas military uniforms. But what caught my eye was the display of flag reproductions showing that each uniform was worn by a soldier fighting for a different government! I saw the entire history of Texas in one quick glance and gained a richer understanding of the state's varied past.

III. Change Exhibits Regularly

Changing exhibits will attract more visitors, especially at museums located in areas that draw repeat seasonal visitors. If people know that the museum will offer something new, they will come again and again. Changing exhibits increases the chances that people who have relatives or friends visiting will bring them to the museum. Faced with the prospect of having to look at the same exhibit over and over again, they may not return. Visitors staying with friends and family accounted for $1.7 billion of the $6.3 billion Wisconsin tourism dollars in 1994 (Davidson-Peterson 1995, 2). Many were repeat visitors, returning to the same place several times in one year.

Exhibit changes require significant effort, but they do not necessarily require extraordinary amounts of cash. The Hermann-Grima House, a historic house in New Orleans, offers tours during the Christmas season. One year, the staff decided to decorate the house as it would have appeared on a 19th-century wedding day. From the museum's collection, they retrieved a wedding dress, examples of appropriate gifts, special tablecloths, and trousseau clothing, which they laid out near the festively decorated bridal bed. They set the dining room table with china and food appropriate for a wedding reception. The exhibit was highly successful. Several bridal magazines featured stories about it, providing the Hermann-Grima House with free publicity all over the southeastern United States.

For their next effort, the museum tried a funeral display. The house was decorated as for a family in mourning. A funeral tour included mannequins in mourning clothes, special dolls for children, and refreshments for guests. The exhibit, a serious historical statement, was based on two years of research. But the out-of-pocket costs were less than $200, primarily for black cloth.

The Ilwaco Heritage Foundation, Ilwaco, Wash., built a reproduction of the town's main street in 1900. The street includes a home, school, church, funeral parlor, barber shop, post office, and saloon. The initial construction was a major and expensive task. But now the small museum has an exhibit that changes every year, with little additional cost, through changing the date in the model town by a decade. While the clothes on the mannequins, posters on the wall, and magazines in the barber shop all change, the desks in the schoolroom can authentically remain the same for half a century. According to the director, summer visitors return each year to see the new interpretation.

IV. Hours

Regular, posted, and publicized opening hours inform visitors and the economic development community that the museum has a professional attitude, even if it is operated by volunteers. Stay open the hours that you have advertised. Few tourists have sufficient interest in a museum to track down a volunteer who will "open on demand." Such an approach may be appropriate for a museum geared only to preserving local objects and sharing them with local residents, but it will not provide access to tourists. A museum with such a limited mission should consider expanding it. When setting hours, a museum should take into account the expense of reprinting brochures and other publicity pieces, as well as the inconvenience and bad publicity caused by outdated and inaccurate materials. Once posted, hours should remain constant as much as possible. Changing them affects not only the museum's literature, but also the information given to tourist and other organizations or published in joint publicity pieces.

Consider the needs of tourists. One Labor Day weekend, I planned a visit to northern Wisconsin as a combination camping trip and museum tour. I drove to a museum I very much wanted to see, only to find it closed. I then remembered that Labor Day always falls on Monday, and many museums in the United States are closed on Mondays. But in northwest Wisconsin and in many other areas, Labor Day closes the summer tourism season. Following the standard operating procedure of closing on Mondays shuts museums' doors on one of the most important days in a very short tourist season.

Museums typically are closed in the evenings when business travelers might welcome doing something other than working or sitting in a hotel room watching television. Many families also look forward to evening entertainment. A museum's potential market may suggest closing a few mornings or afternoons to allow some evening hours. Remember that sports enthusiasts devote themselves to their sport during daylight hours, and will be looking for something to do once the sun sets. A major ski resort recently opened a museum that exhibits the history of the sport. Unfortunately, its 1-4 p.m. hours compete with prime ski time.

Clearly, a director must consider a number of factors before adjusting hours, including staff and volunteer availability and the real demand for visits after hours. A museum attempting to become a more active economic development partner, however, may want to discuss this matter with the local chamber of commerce and visitors bureau.

If a museum is open only during the summer, the director may want to talk to the chamber of commerce about whether opening on certain days during the winter or other seasons, even if for a few hours, would prove helpful. Some chambers of commerce sponsor special weekend festivals or events that might benefit from the added attraction of a reception or other activity at the museum.

When attempting to attract travelers on motor coach tours, attention to hours and timing becomes critical. Tour operators plan their itineraries very carefully. They may need to come half an hour earlier or later than the normal hours in order to fit a museum stop into their schedule. Moreover, buses can be late. If someone on the tour becomes ill, the departure was delayed, or the driver got lost, staff may need to extend the opening hours. One tour operator arrived at a museum 10 minutes late, only to be refused admission. Other operators have encountered clear and unpleasant suggestions that the visitors should hurry because the museum personnel wanted to leave. Although this reaction may be understandable, it does not encourage the tour operator, or his colleagues, to schedule another visit.

V. Make Sure Local People Know About Museum Treasures

Whom do tourists ask when they want to find something? They ask the person with whom they are talking—the hotel desk clerk, gas station attendant, clerk in the corner grocery, or the cashier at the fast food drive-in. When visiting museums in small towns in northwest Wisconsin, I found that townspeople often did not know the location or even the existence of a museum, though it was only half a mile away. Even when a local person knows the location of a museum, he often provides incomplete and confusing directions and inaccurate information about opening hours. Poor directions may get you to your destination, but only if you are familiar with the local, often unmarked, streets. When I was in Oregon City, Oreg., the desk clerk gave me the correct route number, but did not tell me whether to turn north or south.

The problem may be even more profound in larger towns. While on business in Columbus, Ohio, in the late 1980s, I had a three-hour break in the middle of the day. I figured Columbus had to have a good art museum with some good art. But it took two hours and a visit to the chamber of commerce to find out that an art museum did indeed exist, and how to get there.

Sometimes local people know that the museum exists, but have no idea what it contains or why it might interest a visitor. When camping in the Apostle Islands in northern Wisconsin, I took a U.S. Forest Service boat to the camping site. The staff provided a detailed 45-minute lecture on the area and its various islands. The Madeline Island Historical Museum has excellent collections and a first-rate video presentation that illustrates the history of settlement and shipping in the area, all related to the speaker's points. When the boat passed Madeline Island, however, the lecturer merely commented, "There's a museum on the island in case you're interested in that kind of thing."

What can the museum do? Invite local people who are likely to come in contact with potential museum visitors. They may not respond to a regular invitation, but they may bring their children to a holiday event. If the museum provides hospitality training to incoming summer employees, local businesses may send their summer employees to participate. This gets their employees into the museum and provides a chance to inform them about the museum's holdings.

The High Desert Museum, Bend, Oreg., held a community day with admission on a "pay as you wish" basis. According to Marketing and Public Relations Coordinator Aleta Wolin, the museum wanted to "make sure that everyone who lives in the area has seen [the museum. We] hope they will recommend it to others who are visiting, and bring friends and family." The staff wanted to attract newcomers to the community as well as former visitors who did not realize that exhibits changed on a regular basis. They also targeted low-income families, especially those with several children, who found the normal $6.25-per-adult and $3.00-per-child fees a deterrent. The well-publicized event, funded largely by donations from the local business community, drew 1,500 people, approximately 1,000 more than normal daily attendance for that month.

The Cable Natural History Museum, Cable, Wis., has arranged with local realtors to provide a year's annual membership to the museum as a gift to anyone who buys a house. The museum provides the memberships to the realtors at a reduced rate, and the realtors are able to offer their clients an unusual closing gift.

Signs, and other means of identification designed to help tourists, also help local residents. The Hermann-Grima House, New Orleans, can be seen from the famous Bourbon Street, but tourists did not venture through the seedy block in between. The museum tackled this problem by placing a large banner across the front of the building.

The Art Museum of South Texas, located on the waterfront in Corpus Christi, looked similar to adjacent warehouses. The building was constructed by a famous architect who felt that highly visible outside signs would detract from the architectural effect. When the museum placed a 20-foot-square banner across the side of the building where it could be seen by all pleasure boaters, attendance rose. When the banner was removed, attendance fell. The museum now has several banners identifying the museum and its current exhibits.

The art museum's first banner cost $2,000. Karen Venetian, the museum's former assistant educator (now at the Corpus Christi Museum of Science and History), explains that smaller museums could create a banner using staff or volunteer labor and only spend money on materials. Keep the message simple, the lettering large, and use waterproof material for the banner and its lettering.

VI. Share Treasures, Glamour, and Prestige

A. Treasures

What is in the collection that local residents and businesses would find useful? Objects and knowledge. Do people know what kinds of things might be available? Most historical society museums have photographs of the town from previous periods. Restaurants and hotels could use reproductions of those photographs as decoration. Maps and photographs at the museum may provide information that a developer needs to determine the exact location of the flood plain or the site of a hazardous waste dump. Fairlawn, a restored 19th-century mansion in Superior, Wis., provides reproductions of old photographs to local restaurants at a nominal cost. Staff also serve as informal consultants to contractors and interior decorators restoring Victorian homes in the area.

B. Glamour and prestige

Dancing around the dinosaurs is fun! At their annual meetings, both the Texas Association of Museums and the American Association of Museums host cocktail parties and buffet suppers in museums. Food includes regional and ethnic specialties, and there is often entertainment by local dancers. Many museums have settings for parties that can lead to new collaborative and funding opportunities.

The sweeping staircase at the entrance to the Philadelphia Museum of Art makes an impressive setting for corporate entertainment. The museum rents its facilities to its corporate members and to nonprofit organizations for events ranging from board meetings to receptions. According to Mary Jean Huntley, associate for special events, such functions bring "quite a few people to the museum for a relaxed, sophisticated experience [giving them an] understanding of what the museum has to offer."

The French Legation, a historic house in Austin, Tex., rents its garden for events. Someone once threw a reception for the state legislature. The next morning, the director had telephone calls from three state legislators, who thanked her and asked if they could arrange to hold a party for their wives there! Think what a difference this appreciation of historic homes will make the next time the legislature addresses a bill involving historic preservation. Fairlawn rents its lovely facilities for weddings, meetings, and private dinner parties. The fees help the museum's budget, but the director expresses the most enthusiasm for the positive public awareness: "Anyone who comes here once, I . . . consider them an ambassador."

VII. Develop Local Assets

A. Oral history

All communities have people who have participated in historic events. The interpretative center in Stevenson, Wash., includes a video of interviews with five local residents, including a woman who describes her experiences teaching school during the Depression and her life on the home front during World War II. For another wartime exhibit, the Veterans Museum, Madison, Wis., displayed a video of a local World War II veteran who described his feelings during the Battle of Buna in New Guinea. Part of the time the video focused on his face, but mostly, film clips of the battle accompanied his voice. It made the battle vivid, showing how it connected to the experiences of Wisconsin's men.

B. Storytellers

Monica Brei, the public programs coordinator at the State Historical Society of Wisconsin, Madison, uses her background as a children's librarian to incorporate storytelling into the museum's offerings. She provides stories to the museum's guides, and trains them in storytelling. The museum also benefits from the storytelling skills of a retired librarian who provides guide services. In addition to enriching the visitor experience, storytellers can attract new and different audiences, especially ones with ethnic backgrounds. Incorporating storytelling into museums can take a variety of forms. Visitors to the museum's exhibit on fur trading can lift a telephone receiver and listen to a fur trader tell his story. In cooperation with the local school district, the museum hosted a national storytelling conference and sponsored a storyteller-in-residence, who presented programs for children at the museum and in the school classrooms.

A museum searching for storytellers should start with the public library, which will have information about local storytellers and their regional organizations.

C. Craft persons

Many museums provide opportunities for the development of local craft persons. Museum shops provide an outlet for their goods. Museums can deliberately seek out local craft persons by contacting state, regional, and city arts councils and organizations, which often maintain lists of local artists.

Craft persons also can share their skills and increase their income by conducting workshops for the museum. This can lead to increased sales for the institution as well. A museum might actually help to create a marketable skill. At the opening of the End of the Trail Interpretive Center, Oregon City, Oreg., there was a woman selling dolls and pioneer dresses. She told me that she learned how to sew two years ago when she was a volunteer interpreter so that she could make her own costumes. Now she sells costumes on a regular basis.

VIII. Programs, Slide Shows, Video Presentations, and Computer Activities

From an educational point of view, these presentation techniques help fulfill the mission of increasing understanding. From an economic development point of view, they encourage visitation and keep people in the museum longer, making it more likely that they will stay in town for a meal or overnight. Videos and computers have special appeal for younger visitors who grew up with television and learn computer skills at school.

In addition, well-designed programs can more than pay for themselves. The development of a video, slide presentation, or computer program is the type of showy project that often appeals to funders or businesses. They also can help to scale down an elaborate production to a smaller, more effective one. I saw two presentations about the local environment in Washington State: an extremely elaborate and expensive video on Mount St. Helens and a multi-slide presentation on the history of the Columbia Gorge. The latter was actually more enthralling. The excellent slides and the slower presentation allowed the images to sink in, and the script was especially sensitive to the complexities of the local environment.

The Washington State Historical Society's new museum in Tacoma incorporates computers in its exhibits in a major way. A 40-by-60-foot map of Washington is linked to seven computers. Visitors are able to type in a location and watch a television camera move across the map to the designated area. The computer then provides answers to a range of historical and demographic questions about that area. The museum's exhibits contain electronic journals where visitors can access the journals and diaries of historical figures. Such exhibits will appeal especially to individuals with an interest in technology and to visitors with experiential styles of learning, who may not be attracted by the usual historical displays with static written texts. Multimedia presentation techniques permit users to shape their experiences rather than simply respond to a static environment. Visitors select whether to learn a little or a lot about an object, and whether to spend five minutes or an hour investigating a subject.

IX. Sponsor Festivals, Art Fairs, and Concerts

The opening of the Columbia Gorge Interpretive Center, Stevenson, Wash., featured a juried exhibit of local artists' work depicting the Columbia River Gorge. The museum followed this with "Spirit of the Winds," an exhibit by Native American artists. Sales helped the artists, and the art attracted new audiences. Wade House, a historic house in Greenbush, Wis., revived an arts-and-crafts fair in 1987. The show displays only high-quality crafts, handmade in the traditional manner. It grew from 16 exhibitors in 1987, to 125 exhibitors with 4,500 visitors in 1995.

From October through May, the Elvehjem Museum of Art, Madison, Wis., hosts classical music concerts in its largest gallery. These "Sunday Afternoon Live from the Elvehjem" concerts attract several hundred people, and are broadcast live on the state public radio network. During the intermission, the museum's director hosts a discussion about current museum exhibitions. The Los Angeles County Museum of Art remains open on Friday evenings, combining free jazz concerts in the entrance plaza with an opportunity to purchase refreshments and a light supper. Forts Folle Avoine, Siren, Wis., hosts an annual July event with costumed historical re-enactors from all over the country, who camp on its grounds for a week. Everything in the camp represents the period between 1680 and 1840. The event has grown from 57 to 110 camp sites in four years, with 3,500 attending during a single weekend.

X. Be a Part of the Local Team

The extent and exact nature of a museum's participation in local affairs is determined by its mission and staff abilities. Museum leaders can set limits, but if they want to be considered a part of the local team, they will need to contribute time and money. Join the local chamber of commerce; buy an ad in its chief promotion piece. Sponsor a booth at the local fair. If the director does not have time to attend the key business-related service club, one of the board members already may be a member. Perhaps she would represent the museum and keep museum personnel informed about the club's activities.

Often a museum's hesitation comes more from lack of vision or flexibility than from lack of resources. In one small town, a museum director complained bitterly that the chamber of commerce would not purchase a $50 museum membership even though the museum attracted so many tourists. The director of the chamber of commerce responded that the museum would not buy a $50 ad in the annual publicity piece, even though it attracted people to the museum! Each director gave reasons why he could not contribute, including "if we contributed to them, we'd have to contribute to everything in town." A clear

cooperative statement of mutual support and some flexibility
would have enabled them to work out an exchange pleasing to
their boards and supporters.

XI. Target the Market and Market to the Target

A museum needs to address two different considerations si-
multaneously. Based on mission and collection, who is the most
likely and who is the chosen audience? Whom is the local
tourist industry attempting to attract? Are these two target
markets the same? Is there an overlap? Chapter 4 discusses
marketing in more detail.

XII. Think About the Visitor (Customer)

As museums expand their markets and come under rising pressure to operate in a business-like fashion, visitor satisfaction
will become more important. Management techniques that
build strong teams and eliminate waste will be noticed. Some
science and technology centers have demonstrated leadership
in adopting such business management practices as conducting
visitor surveys and adopting a team approach to management.
If professionally conducted surveys seem too expensive, talk to
a marketing professor at your local college to see if the museum's needs can dovetail with potential student projects (see the
discussion on surveys in chapter 4).

But the real key is to mobilize the entire organization to view
customer service as vital, according to Roy Shafer, past president and CEO of the Ohio Center of Science & Industry
(COSI), Columbus. Shafer is now principal, Roy L. Shafer Co.,
a company that offers strategies for organizational change. He
points out that all museum personnel either serve the customer
(visitor) directly or serve someone who is serving customers.
COSI developed a game plan to identify how to ensure that
every individual who comes in contact with the institution receives good service. Floor teams include staff from exhibits,

programs, and support services, all wearing the COSI team "look"—a polo shirt or sweatshirt with the COSI logo. Each team member, from those on the front-line to those normally behind the scenes, including the CEO, wears the shirts while at work. And each one hosts visitors on a regular basis. Once a month, the team members spend time performing the task of other personnel, such as learning how to clean Plexiglas or trying to match invoices with purchase orders. They learn directly that each person's performance affects overall product and customer satisfaction. The museum also has an annual bonus award system called Performance Plus, in which customer service is a major factor.

The Mint Museum of Art in Charlotte, N.C., benefited from outstanding customer service in an unexpected manner. The curator of decorative arts spends one afternoon a week answering questions and evaluating people's collections. One day, a woman phoned to inquire about reading materials and about glazed ceramics in the Mint's collection. She called again several months later, and again four months after that. When she invited the curator to visit her collection of tin-glazed ware, he accepted immediately. Impressed both by the curator's knowledge and the way he responded to her, the woman offered her 32-piece ceramics collection to the the Mint, an addition that fills gaps in the museum's 1,600-piece collection of European ceramics. The collector had called a number of museums on the East Coast, quietly making similar inquiries, before selecting the place where she felt her collection would be most valued and that best disseminated information about ceramics.

Learn from other nonprofits. While visiting small museums in one state, I found that more than a third of the directors were concerned about their volunteers or board members. Typical complaints included board members who lacked understanding of the museum's curatorial role, volunteers who were unreliable or started projects that did not correspond with museum priorities, and trustees unwilling to change antiquated exhibits. The bibliography lists several publications that deal with the special management problems of museums and other nonprofits.

References

Davidson-Peterson Associates, Inc. *The Economic Impact of Expenditures by Tourists on Wisconsin.* York, Maine: Davidson-Peterson Associates, Inc., 1995.

Neal, Arminta. *Help for the Small Museum: Handbook of Exhibit Ideas and Methods,* 2nd ed. Boulder, Colo.: Pruett Publishing Company, 1987.

Marketing the Museum

I. Identifying the Target Market

A. The museum's purpose

Marketing a museum involves more than placing an ad in a big city newspaper. A sound marketing program may not even rely on newspaper advertising.

Proper marketing starts with a re-reading of the museum's mission statement. Whom does *this* museum serve? Does it exist primarily as a source of pride for the town's residents, or to promote historical understanding among school children? Does it attract occasional visitors from a nearby city for special events, or does it have a collection that merits national and international attention? Does the museum have as many visitors as it can handle, yet need more financial support from local government or the business community? Before you design a marketing plan, ensure that trustees, staff, and key volunteers have an answer—and the same answer—to the following question: What does this museum try to sell and to whom? The market should not drive the mission nor should a museum's direction change with every market fluctuation, but museums make a mistake by ignoring market realities.

In the question, What does the museum sell and to whom?, the *what* represents the product. This product might be pride in the community, a chance to experience a representative collection of world art, or an understanding of state history. *Whom,* in business terms, refers to customers—generally visitors or patrons, but it also could mean county or city council members. Businesses often divided customers into market segments. A museum's typical market segments include drop-in visitors, school groups, attendees at special events, motor coach tours, and others. Successful selling to each of those market segments usually depends on very different approaches.

The first step in developing a market plan is to start with a clear statement of what the museum "sells" and to whom. Many museums now are attempting to increase tourist visitation, reasoning that they have penetrated local markets and that tourism offers the best area for rapid growth.

B. Trends

1. Tourism, a growing industry

Travel is a $6-billion industry, and is responsible for creating almost 16 million jobs. In 1995, 1.2 billion people made personal trips, an increase of 3 percent from 1994 (Tourism Works for America Council 1996). The travel industry ranks as the third-largest United States retail industry and its second-largest employer.

2. Tourism turns gray

Although most travelers are now between 35 and 54 years old, the average age of travelers will increase as this group ages. In 1996, the first baby boomers turned 50. This means that one-fourth of the U.S. population has already reached 50, a proportion that will increase to one-third by 2020. People have their greatest discretionary income during their 50s and 60s, making them prime prospects as museum visitors, gift shop customers, and donors.

Slightly more than 60 percent of older people contribute to a non-religious charity every year. Mature adults travel more than younger ones and for longer periods of time. A study conducted for the American Association of Retired Persons (AARP) found that although approximately one-third of older travelers tend to go to the same places again and again, one-fourth look for new places, and another 40 percent try new places at least occasionally (American Association of Retired Persons 1992).

Older adults are interested in health issues, current events, history, and art. The AARP study found that learning new things ranked fifth on their list of leisure priorities. And their ability to travel off-season provides another reason for museums to reach out to older people.

Implications for museums:

Will older visitors find the museum user-friendly?

Many older people use bifocal glasses and hearing aids. Do signs, labels, brochures, and audio-tour equipment meet those needs, or is the print too small and the equipment too hard to use? Many have mobility problems. Do the parking facilities accommodate their needs? Is there parking for disabled visitors nearby? Does the museum have benches or chairs comfortable enough for someone with arthritis?

a. Is the museum an inviting place to take grandchildren?
More than 70 percent of older people have grandchildren. During any one month, 11 million grandparents take trips to see grandchildren, another 20 million send them a greeting card, and 24 million buy them a gift. This intergenerational ac-

tivity opens enormous program and attendance possibilities for museums. Exhibits or activities that are appropriate for grand-children and grandparents to enjoy together, always important, become especially relevant during summer vacations and Christmas and Thanksgiving holidays. In 1994, 50 million adults reported that they planned a summer trip with children or grandchildren.

Does the museum appeal to several generations? Living history programs enliven past events for people of all ages. A visitor to Forts Folle Avoine, Siren, Wis., reported that her nephews stomped rice to loosen the hulls and tried their hands at throw-ing hatchets into a log. The 12- and 16-year-old boys found the experience fascinating, she said, "and you know how hard it is to interest [teen-agers] in anything." At the Madeline Island Historical Museum, LaPointe, Wis., visitors can feel the differ-ence among fox, beaver, and coyote furs, as well as the texture of a finished beaver hat. The 19th-century furniture at Wade House, Greenbush, Wis., must be protected from constant handling by visitors. But children and adults can carry candles to the upstairs bedrooms, thus experiencing the reality of life without electricity. Children also are allowed to climb on one bed, which is covered with a modern reproduction of a 19th-century quilt, and feel the texture of a corn husk mattress. And everyone enjoys the cider that is produced from apples cranked by young visitors.

b. Does the museum want to capture the bus tour market?
According to the American Bus Association (ABA), a motor coach with a full load of 43 passengers can provide between $5,000 and $7,000 to a community during an overnight stay. This includes money spent on hotels, meals, admission fees, and shopping. The National Tour Association estimates that tours using all forms of transportation spent $8.6 billion in 1995 (Tourism Works for America Council 1996). The ABA

says that 37 percent of the charters and tours market, including local groups on day trips, consists of school groups; another 37 percent comprises visitors ages 55 and older. The adults tend to be educated and have incomes averaging $41,400 (author's conversation with ABA staff).

If a museum wants to enter this growing market, it should examine its operation carefully to determine whether it can appropriately serve these audiences, and develop a plan for attracting tours. The potential benefits are there, but they usually take three to five years to realize.

c. Does the museum provide special programs for older visitors?

Many museums provide special programs for older people. Some museums partner with Elderhostel programs. Usually, the museum sponsors program attendees, arranging for 22-1/2 hours of instruction over a five- to six-day period, as well as for housing, food, and entertainment. The national Elderhostel organization markets the program through a quarterly catalog that is sent to more than half a million people. People on this list are an ideal market for museums. Primarily retired professionals who either have participated in an Elderhostel program or requested the catalog, they match the profile of those most likely to visit museums. The program also provides opportunities for partnering with local educational institutions for both faculty and housing, as well as with local motels, restaurants, and entertainment attractions.

d. Does the museum have a marketing strategy that appeals to the older tourist?

A number of organizations have developed successful strategies for marketing to older people. Successful approaches include depicting older people as attractive, active, doing things with other people, and enjoying themselves. AARP has an ex-

cellent "info-pak" on older consumers that includes demographic data, preference and interest information, a pamphlet
called *How to Advertise to Maturity*, and a short, well-annotat-
ed bibliography. Contact: American Association of Retired Persons, 601 E St. N.W., Washington, DC 20049; 202/434-2277.

3. Short trips
Tourism has shifted from the traditional annual two-week vacation to more frequent, shorter trips. Weekend trips accounted
for half of all trips in 1993 (U.S. Travel Data Center, *1994 Travel Market Report,* 1995). Dual income families often lack time
even for normal housekeeping chores. Scheduling a long vacation becomes difficult when a family must juggle two work
schedules. Many families also lack funds for longer trips.

The trend towards shorter trips, closer to home, provides opportunities for museums to collaborate with hotels and restaurants to promote weekend getaway holidays. The Art Institute
of Chicago, for example, cooperates with hotels that offer
weekend packages including tickets to exhibits. During a Mon-
et exhibit, one hotel sold all its weekend packages more than a
month before the exhibit closed. Partnering with hotels also
might prove successful for smaller, rural museums located in
restful countrysides.

4. Tourism is more international
The increasing interdependence of the world's economy, de-
creasing air fares, fluctuations in exchange rates, and greater
incomes for residents of many countries have increased international tourism. International travel is America's largest export. According to the Tourism Works for America Council,
foreign visitors now spend more than $79.7 billion a year in the
United States (Tourism Works for America Council 1996). Foreign visitors account for a significant percent of the entire
United States tourism business, and they spend more money
and time than domestic travelers.

Implications for museums:
Surveys of international travelers show that visiting historic places ranks fifth in their leisure activities, after shopping, eating in restaurants, sightseeing in cities, and sunbathing. Visiting art galleries/museums and national parks ties for seventh place (U.S. Travel and Tourism Administration, *In-Flight Survey,* 1995). Museums desiring to reach these visitors may be able to obtain useful data about where tourists enter the country, where they visit, and projections for visitation from various countries from the Travel Industry Association, 1100 New York Ave. N.W., Suite 450 West, Washington, DC 20005; 202/408-8422.

More than half of the states operate tourism offices abroad, and even more advertise in foreign markets (Ketterer 1990, 26). Your state tourism program probably can provide information about foreign visitors who might have an interest in your museum, as well as suggestions for the best way to include it as an attraction in promotions done by the state or other groups.

5. Tourism is more segmented

Today, the mass market is divided into several specialized segments. Wisconsin's Department of Tourism surveyed people who called its 800-number requesting information about the state. After extensive interviews, the research firm divided potential visitors to the state into types, based on a number of demographic factors and differences in tastes and interests. These types were described as fulfilled people, actualizers, strivers, experiencers, and believers.

Fulfilled people
Basic characteristics:
    30-55 years old
    moderate household income
    white-collar professional, manager, or retired

> college-educated
> have older children
> are "comfortable, satisfied"

Fulfilled people like art and culture; value history and education; and go to museums, zoos, historical sites, theatrical performances, and classical music concerts. They enjoy reading,
antiquing, and photography, and participate in such sports as
sailing, hiking, golf, tennis, swimming, and downhill and cross-
country skiing. They want variety in vacations and value environmental conservation, education, history, and art and culture. The best ways to reach this group are through
newspapers, public affairs and prime-time television programs,
and home and garden, food, and general interest magazines.

Actualizers
Basic characteristics:
> 30-55 years old
> high-income households
> white-collar workaholics
> well-educated
> two-income households
> teen-age children
> are broadminded
> like to be in control

This group goes to museums, zoos, theatrical performances,
and classical music concerts. Actualizers enjoy photography,
reading, and antiquing. In addition to the sports liked by the
fulfilled group, they also enjoy bicycling, water skiing, and
horseback riding. They are ardent newspaper readers, but are
less likely to watch television. When they do, they favor informational programs. They read business, food, and special interest magazines.

Strivers
Basic characteristics:
   25-44 years old
   moderate household income
   clerical, blue-collar, service occupations
   high school graduate
   either married with children or single
   family-oriented
   want to be big spenders
   are trend conscious
   are easily bored

Unlikely to visit museums, this group prefers spectator sports, camping, state fairs, zoos, theme parks, and water parks. Strivers prefer watching television to reading, and when they read, choose weekly tabloids and human interest stories.

Experiencers
Basic characteristics:
   18-35 years old
   low to moderate household income
   entry-level, white-collar workers
   have not yet completed their formal education
   single, never married
   highly disposable incomes
   self-centered socializers
   follow fashion and fads

This group tends to select vacations with variety, thrills, and strenuous physical activity. Experiencers watch television action and sitcom shows, listen to the radio, and read sports, fashion, and men's magazines.

Believers
Basic characteristics:
   45-66 years old

low household income
homemakers and retired blue-collar workers
high school education or less
married or widowed, with grandchildren
patriotic
enjoy a settled routine, avoid risk

Believers like to spend vacations visiting friends and relatives.
They like predictability and simple, unstructured activities
such as walking outdoors. They gamble at casinos, but carefully limit the amount of money that they risk. They watch television frequently, and are light readers of retirement, home and
garden, and general interest magazines.

The study revealed which groups were most likely to visit various Wisconsin counties, based on people living in surrounding
states, kinds of ads most likely to appeal to each group, and the
best media for reaching them. Talk to local marketing experts
about how demographic and life style characteristics might
help you identify and target your best prospects.

Identifying demographic characteristics may also encourage a
museum to re-examine its basic mission. When the study's
findings were presented to a group of museums in northwest
Wisconsin, one museum director loudly articulated his disin-
terest in attracting more actualizers and fulfilled people, since
they already used museums. Instead, he wanted to attract more
people from the other categories, people who did not currently
visit his museum.

However, museums attempting to increase visitation may benefit most by marketing to the fulfilled and actualizer groups. If a
museum wants to expand the intellectual and cultural horizons
of the other groups, it should think carefully about the best
method. Encouraging visits from actualizers, and then using
the resulting funds for special school programs for the children

from all groups, may prove more cost-effective than trying to convince adults of all types to visit the museum.

If a museum does want to attract all types, it will need appropriately designed exhibits and activities as well as special marketing approaches. Experiencers do not want to look at, read about, or listen to a lecture about an object; they want to experience it. For example, the USS Silversides & Maritime Museum, Muskegon, Mich., offers visitors the opportunity to spend a night on the submarine: "Eat in the mess, sleep in the bunks, and live as the submarine sailors did during World War II."

Technology interests experiencers, many of whom can be reached via the Internet. An exhibit on the techniques of restoring an historic building would be of more interest to this group than touring the house's elegant rooms. They like science museums, especially ones that emphasize high technology and use interactive exhibits and videos. Experiencers might visit the Washington State Historical Society, Tacoma, which includes a map connected to a computer that invites a user to move a pointer to her home town and then find out about its history.

Believers, who are interested in both walking and ecology, might visit the Cable Natural History Museum, Cable, Wis., which sponsors an outdoor walking tour. They also might like exhibits that appeal to their patriotism, such as the extensive exhibit on the 50th anniversary of World War II held at the Wisconsin Maritime Museum, Manitowoc. The museum and local veterans groups co-sponsored a dance that recreated a 1946 celebration for returning veterans. On the other hand, strivers would be attracted by a sports exhibit. When marketing to these two groups, stress value and use discounts and coupons.

Another study, an in-depth analysis of the visitors at the Henry

Ford Museum & Greenfield Village, Dearborn, Mich., emphasized the differences between sophisticated and non-sophisticated visitors. The study indicated that visitors with the highest educational and professional levels approached their visits differently than those with blue-collar jobs and less education. The more sophisticated visitors focused on the objects or exhibits that particularly interested them, ignoring orientation videos and tours. Other visitors, less comfortable with museums, wanted directions to the high points, suggestions about how to view the exhibits, and short labels written at a 10th-grade level that assumed no prior knowledge of the subject.

Canadian-based Lord Cultural Resources Planning and Management, Inc., developed projections for Ontario that illustrate the benefits for museums that market broadly. The study showed that approximately 15 percent of potential visitors to Ontario plan their trip around the city's cultural events. Another 30 percent think about cultural attractions when making their travel decisions. The other 65 percent of visitors do not think about cultural attractions when making trip decisions, but 40 percent of them said they might participate in a cultural event if it was convenient (Lord 1993).

If a museum wishes to attract as many tourists as possible, increase its visitation rates and income, and make its programming more effective, it should first market to the 15 percent who are seriously interested, and then to the 30 percent who are somewhat interested. If your mission includes broadening the cultural horizons of people visiting your area, determine how to modify the museum product so it appeals to them. Or combine it with another event or activity, such as a festival.

II. How to Find Market Information

After identifying a target audience and taking into consideration how changing national trends might influence its potential size, how can a museum access more specific data on where to locate potential visitors? Analyze current customers. From a marketing viewpoint, learning about current visitors can help in several ways. Turning current visitors into repeaters expands visitation. One marketing expert says that "it costs five times as much to sell to a new customer" than an existing one (Levinson 1993, 28). Expanding the market to people who fit the profile of current visitors will prove more cost effective and easier than attracting an entirely different audience. Finally, clearly articulating the differences between visitors and nonvisitors can show whether the museum needs new marketing approaches or special efforts.

A. Who are the existing customers?

What if a museum has not generated any information about its visitors? Most of the smaller museums in northwest Wisconsin and southwest Washington do not collect data on where their visitors live. Forts Folle Avoine, Siren, Wis., is one of the few that has reliable addresses, complete with zip codes. Most museums put their guest books by the front desk in full view of a volunteer or staff member, says Director Edgar Oerichbauer. "If I walked into your museum and you treated me insensitively, I wouldn't want to write that with you looking over my shoulder," he says. Forts Folle Avoine's guest book is in an area where no staff can see what visitors are writing, near a bulletin board with listings of museum events and a rack with tourism information about the state. These informational areas attract visitors on their way into or out of the museum. About 35 percent also stop and sign the guest book.

According to Oerichbauer, many museums have "glitzy books with one line . . . a book that you would find at a wedding reception." Such books discourage people from making comments or providing a full address, he says. By contrast, half of the signers of Forts Folle Avoine's book provide comments,

and 90 percent give their full addresses. The addresses tell
Oerichbauer where his advertising works and where it does
not. And based on the theory "if they came once, they'll come
again," the data also provides a mailing list for annual events.
In addition, staff review the mostly favorable comments, paying special heed to the suggestions and complaints that come
from 5 percent of the signers.

Data about visitors form the essential base for marketing, planning, and public relations purposes. Every museum should develop a means to obtain this information. One expert says that
"analysis of attendance records is the most accurate and reliable measurement of the market for museums" (Silberberg
1991, 57). Properly designed, a simple form for recording daily
attendance can provide data on such variables as the ages of
visitors; weather conditions; times, days, and weeks of highest
attendance; visitors to special events; school visits and bus
tours; and, at the very least, zip codes.

With minimal effort, zip codes can be recorded when tickets
are sold. The National Aquarium in Baltimore uses a cash reg-
ister that enables ticket sellers to record address information
when ringing up the sale. The ticket seller at the Wisconsin
Maritime Museum, Manitowoc, merely jots down the information on the half of the ticket that the museum keeps.

Zip codes contain a wealth of information. A number of information service companies compile statistics from the U.S. Bureau of the Census, consumer surveys, and other sources for
data on the characteristics of residents for every zip code in the
nation. These companies normally sell this data to businesses,
but similar information can be found in publications. For example, CACI Marketing Systems publishes *The Sourcebook of
Zip Code Demographics,* which identifies residents most likely
to buy certain products, and places people into one of 13 consumer categories. Using this book, a museum could determine

whether its visitors came from an area of predominantly "prosperous older couples," "newly formed households," or "young, frequent movers." Your local public library might have a copy of the sourcebook; the information is also available on various computer data networks.

Using zip codes can result in inaccurate data if the demography of an area changes or if the boundaries of the zip codes shift. Ask a successful local business person who uses market research to serve as an adviser to the museum, and assist the staff person, board member, or intern conducting the analysis. Another good source is the nearest public or university library with a government documents reference librarian. These librarians, trained to locate and interpret the data in government documents, have detailed data from the Census Bureau and other government agencies, usually in both printed and computer disk form.

Museums also can group together the zip codes of the largest number of visitors. By locating the county that visitors live in or near, a museum can determine whether to send announcements to the daily newspapers, suburban shoppers guides, or other media. The National Aquarium in Baltimore found zip code research helpful when requesting financial support from the city and four adjacent counties. It justified funding requests by detailing to each county how many of its residents used the aquarium.

B. Surveys

If collecting data from each visitor is neither feasible nor reliable, a museum can conduct periodic surveys. Even museums that do collect basic visitor data should conduct occasional visitor surveys, which provide additional information and supplement the self-reported visitor information. Before undertaking any survey, however, the museum should answer two fundamental questions: How will the museum use the information?

and How can it ensure that this survey produces both valid and reliable results?

Answering the first question carefully will shape the design of the survey and obviate the need for a second survey to glean additional information, notes H. Nicholas Muller, III, president and CEO, Frank Lloyd Wright Foundation, Scottsdale, Ariz. Besides delaying projects, repeating surveys costs money and vexes respondents. If the intent is to convince the county council to continue funding because museum visitation benefits local businesses, the survey should determine how many visitors come from outside the community, their incomes, and how much money they spend locally. On the other hand, a museum seeking an educational foundation grant for a program to increase its attractiveness to minorities requires data on race and ethnicity. In designing the survey, ask staff, trustees, and key volunteers, "What decisions might we make differently if we knew x?" After crafting the survey questions, read each one carefully, asking, "If the answer to this question were x, how would that affect the museum's policy or actions?" If the answer will not provide any guidance for future actions, do not ask the question, or reword it so the answers will be relevant.

The survey should be valid and reliable. Ensure that the survey reflects what the museum needs and targets visitors of various backgrounds at different times of the day and year to ensure that results are meaningful. The individuals who answer the questionnaire should represent the average visitor, not the exception. For example, the Henry Ford Museum & Greenfield Village, Dearborn, Mich., conducted an audience study that found that widows visiting during the winter months were not the same widows who visited other times of the year. If the surveyor had interviewed only winter visitors, the data for widows would have been misleading.

If no one on the museum staff has expertise in survey research, consult a marketing expert or a sociologist at a local college. Talking to staff at other museums of similar size or browsing through the methodology books in the sociology section of a university bookstore also might prove useful.

C. Focus groups

Convening focus groups is another approach that helps to determine what factors might increase visitation. Asking current visitors to discuss why they came, whether and why they plan to return, and the reasons why their friends do not visit the museum can provide valuable information. Focus groups also can suggest issues to explore and other sources of statistical information. From 1987 to 1989, the Getty Center for Education in the Arts and the J. Paul Getty Museum, Malibu, Calif., sponsored a study in which 11 art museums held a series of focus groups with staff, visitors, and non-visitors. The results helped the museums to re-examine missions, attract non-visitors, and develop interpretive materials and educational programming.

Sophisticated focus groups such as those convened by major manufacturers testing an ad campaign, or even the Getty study, are far more elaborate and expensive than most museums can afford. However, you can incorporate the same principles in a less extensive application. As in a survey, identify the participants, ask staff, board members, and trustees to develop questions, and analyze the questions carefully. The focus group should be conducted by someone with good facilitating skills, who is familiar with the basic how-to books on the subject. The discussion can be audio-taped and transcribed rather than video-taped. Video-taping might prove disconcerting to participants and should be done from behind a one-way window, if possible. The focus group's validity and reliability begin with the composition of the participating group, the appropriateness of the questions asked, and a good analysis of the results.

A museum also can conduct focus groups to determine how to attract non-visitors. The Getty project's professional interviewers asked participants to provide names of non-visitors with certain demographic characteristics, including at least a high school diploma, annual family incomes of $25,000 or more, and, for some cities, a certain racial or ethnic background. A museum should develop criteria for selection that will provide participants similar to those in the target audience. If you cannot afford professional recruiters, consider whether people with characteristics similar to those desired might be willing to assist. For example, would members of an African-American sorority participate? A labor union? A professional society of architects? Your museum could use its zip code data to locate neighborhoods with high concentrations of the people it wishes to contact. Or it could arrange a trade with a neighborhood association, perhaps allowing the group to hold its next volunteer thank-you party at the museum.

D. Use data from other organizations

In addition to gaining information about potential future markets from visitors and non-visitors, museums may find that other community or state organizations have data useful for analyzing market potential. Museums with similar collections or locations may have data about their visitors that might predict likely responses from your potential audience. Nearby museums with different types of collections also may have conducted useful analyses of the geographic area's demographics.

The Wisconsin Department of Tourism not only analyzes the types of people requesting information about visiting the state, and their interests, but also keeps track of the callers who visit the area. In addition, the department collects data about visitor spending, necessary for determining visitors' economic impact.

The departments of economic development or tourism in other states also collect data about tourism and its potential. Museums in the few states that do not have this data should look to an adjacent state for assistance. In addition, local chambers of commerce and economic development organizations may have relevant information. States participating in the National Trust for Historic Preservation's Main Street program often have solid local data (see chapter 5 for more information about this program). Museums should invest some time locating existing data before spending considerably more time and money collecting it themselves.

III. Developing a Marketing Plan

A. Goals

Having determined the target audiences, the museum can design a marketing plan to attract them. A simple museum marketing plan usually contains five general components: (1) specific goals, (2) objectives, (3) strategies, (4) a timetable, and (5) measurement, also called evaluation. The development of the plan should involve all of the key actors in a museum. Solid marketing, like the tip of an iceberg, rests on a broad and deep institutional base, much of it unseen. Everybody working or volunteering for the museum and its board should be familiar with and have a copy of the final written plan.

Marketing plans also require at least an annual revision. A plan does not have to be long, but it should be written. This avoids or greatly reduces misunderstandings or disagreements that may emerge when projects get underway. Otherwise, problems that surface during program implementation may hurt feelings, erode cooperation, and lead to wrong or inappropriate information being given to individuals or the media.

The process of stating specific goals will force everyone to agree on target markets and the reasons for attracting different visitors. In 1993, the Mint Museum of Art, Charlotte, N.C., launched a five-year plan whose goals included "To reach individuals or groups from outside the traditional definition of museum audiences, and implement the strategy of the 'museum as a refuge,' which makes access to the collection and staff consultation available to organizations that deal with senior citizens, non-traditional families, people with disabilities, or people with serious illnesses, to make use of the contemplative, social and healing aspects of art in addition to the typical focus on aesthetic issues." Thereafter, this museum, internationally known for its ceramics collection, could appropriately mount a major exhibit about HIV/AIDS, which presented life masks and oral histories.

A museum might establish different sets of goals, objectives, strategies, and measurements for its target audiences, whether they be local community leaders, schoolchildren, summer cottage owners, tourists, specific minority groups, or geographic areas. The Texas Association of Museums developed an outstanding publication called *Action Plan: Multicultural Initiatives in Texas Museums,* which has suggestions for attracting diverse audiences and includes case studies, ideas for partnering with diverse community groups, and an extraordinarily sensitive glossary that lists words least likely to cause offense.

Marketing goals may vary for each type of visitor, as with the actualizers and experiencers identified in the Wisconsin research. Objectives might change with the seasons. For example, towns in southwest Washington need to attract more visitors during early spring and late autumn, times of unpredictable weather. As part of this effort, four museums in the area collaborated on a brochure called "Rain or Shine."

Reaching multiple audiences, often a necessity for a museum, also may create marketing pitfalls. Sending different messages to different groups, for example, may dilute the impact of one facet of a marketing effort. You also run the risk of sending conflicting messages. In *Guerrilla Marketing,* Jay Conrad Levinson urges businesses to center their efforts around one core idea. He tells clients to write out the idea using as many words as necessary, and then reduce it to seven sentences, and then seven words. If museum staff cannot do that, they may not clearly understand the mission.

If a museum does stand for several different ideas, do they complement each other or do they conflict? Are different staff members promoting different core ideas? What is the appropriate balance for the various priorities? Does the staff agree on the idea but not on the message or the appropriate medium? How can you ensure that all elements of your marketing plan support the museum's goals?

B. Product mix and positioning

The four elements of the traditional business marketing plan include product, place, promotion, and price. Often, museums have more control over these elements than they realize. To develop a marketing plan, you should understand how to employ and modify each of these elements so that they best support your marketing goals.

Product mix and positioning are two business approaches useful for museums considering how to make themselves more attractive to the desired audience. Mark Lane, then director of the Witte Museum, San Antonio, Tex., noting the changing demographics of the museum's neighborhood, was determined to alter the existing approach, which primarily targeted children. He instituted a series of lectures and tours that tapped the interests of young professionals and older, childless couples, thereby expanding the museum's clientele.

The opposite approach was taken by Robert A. Kret, director

of the Leigh Yawkey Woodson Museum, Wausau, Wis. He
wanted to attract more families and encourage them to visit
again and again. Staff created a "Kids' Club" based on children's attraction to baseball cards. Each month, club members
who visit the museum obtain a card with a picture of a museum object on one side and information about it on the other.
The museum provides workbooks with activities based on each
month's trading card. Club members also receive a free membership to the museum, attend regular club meetings, and receive a newsletter with advance notice of new exhibits and other activities for children. Visitation has jumped 20 to 25
percent. According to Kret, the "kids take ownership." Instead
of parents "dragging their kids" to the museum, now children
are "dragging their parents."

A museum should consider each of its services as a separate
product: exhibits; workshops; special events; the store; even
the different aspects of an exhibit, such as the paintings and
the video presentation about the artist's life. Each of these
"products" will appeal to different segments of the potential
market. All museums have some product mix. The museum
should consciously understand and consider its product mix as
part of its marketing strategy so that its events support the
overall marketing goals and objectives. Otherwise, the museum
will bear the expenses of a product mix without being able to
maximize its potential benefits.

Museums can plan events that appeal to diverse audiences and
schedule them during the most appropriate hours. Exhibits
also can be developed or timed as part of a marketing approach. When the Memphis Pink Palace Museum and Plane-
tarium, Memphis, Tenn., learned that the "Ramses the Great"
exhibit hosted by the city would not display any mummies, the
museum developed a complementary exhibit on the process
and religious significance of mummification and the scientific

methods used to learn about it. Attendance at the Memphis Pink Palace Museum exhibit benefited from the extensive publicity the city provided for the "Ramses" event.

The appropriate product mix depends upon the museum's mission and on how it seeks to position itself in the marketplace. In business terms, a museum—except during school visits—is part of the leisure-time market. It competes with every other activity a potential visitor might choose during her leisure time. A museum should understand its current position within the leisure-time market, and consider where it wishes to be. Is the museum a viable alternative to a theme park, taking a history class at a community college, reading a book on the history of science, or watching a television program on ecology? How does attendance at the museum compare to that of other museums in the city or area? How does attendance compare to similar museums in different cities? If the museum does not attract audiences as large as those at others in the area or with similar collections, what are those museums doing that results in their greater success?

Whatever your mission statement, determining which activities fulfill the needs of your desired audience will identify who is competing with you for their time, energy, and money. Once you identify the competition, you can better determine how to position the museum as something slightly different, with better quality, service, and price.

C. Place

Most museums have little option regarding location. However, they can reduce the negative aspects of an existing location or building appearance. One museum, which looked similar to adjacent warehouses on the waterfront, distinguished itself by placing a large banner across the wall facing the river. The graphics constantly reminded sailors and other pleasure boaters that the building housed exhibits of potential interest to them. Visitors to the Smithsonian Institution, Washington, D.C., can arrange to have guards escort them to their cars after late evening programs, alleviating concerns about parking in an area that is often deserted at night.

Think about the positive aspects, such as the grounds and any other potential locations for receptions, parties, or similar events. Staff at historic houses and other museums can learn from the public relations and marketing efforts of Biltmore Estate, a privately owned historic home in Asheville, N.C. Biltmore regularly publicizes the flowers that bloom in its extensive garden. Visitors return again and again to see the garden during different seasons. Commercial photographers use the gardens as background for their models, and the catalogues in which the photographs appear often cite Biltmore Estate. Film crews also use the grounds and house as a scenic backdrop. Film credits mentioning the estate provide further publicity.

Another marketing approach incorporates off-site exhibits or traveling vans, which extend a museum's reach to any venue it may deem appropriate. The Maryhill Museum of Art, Goldendale, Wash., presented an exhibit of objects from its Native American collection at Skamania Lodge, a golf resort and conference center in a nearby town. Approximately 20 objects, displayed with proper care and security, illustrated how the region's Native Americans used local plants and animals as inspiration for the designs on pottery and other objects. The exhibit included an invitation to visit the museum, which indicated both its location and a description of its holdings.

A van from the Carson County Square House Museum, Panhandle, Tex., takes slide shows and trunk programs to schools within a 150-mile radius. The trunks contain real artifacts and provide students with a variety of educational activities. The pioneer trunk focuses on the hardship of a pioneer journey, and students pack a wagon, which encourages them to carefully consider the importance of each object to pioneer life. Another trunk contains a calendar made from animal hide, which was used by the Kiowas to record their history from 1863 to 1892. It illustrates how people used symbols rather than written words to record events. Other trunks contain objects on the history of the Plains Indians, the Spanish influence on ranching, and ways Christmas is celebrated around the world. The outreach program reaches 1,000 teachers and 15,000 students annually, compared to 5,000 on-site visitors.

D. Promotion

Promotion includes anything and everything the museum does to let people know that it exists, why they should come, why they should support it, and why they should take pride in its role in their community. In business, promotion traditionally includes public relations and paid advertising.

Again, the first step involves defining goals and creating a plan for reaching the specific audience indicated in the marketing plan. Simply obtaining increased newspaper coverage does not necessarily do the job. Which newspapers reach the desired audience? Would radio be a better medium? Should a museum use flyers, brochures, bus cards, buttons, or other devices? How much free promotion can a museum generate? The museum should develop the most cost-effective strategy given its budget and staff skills.

State departments of tourism or economic development may provide free materials, research, or technical assistance. The Wisconsin Department of Tourism has completed an analysis of the state's best potential tourism markets and has developed strategies for the best way to reach them, including which newspapers and magazines to target. For a little more than $5, they will provide 1,000 zip-sorted mailing labels with addresses of people who have contacted the department for publications such as brochures on heritage and historic sites. This mailing list seems tailor-made for history museums within the appropriate areas.

The tourism department publishes a biannual auto-tour book, both a fall/winter and a spring/summer recreation guide, and calendar of events. In 1996, for example, the department sent its fall booklet to 115,000 people, including Wisconsin residents and out-of-state tourists. The department also cooperates with the Wisconsin Association of Convention and Visitors Bureaus, which publishes a "Go To It Guide." In the spring and fall of 1996, the tourism department mailed the guide to 240,000 travelers from Wisconsin and other states. Placing information about the museum and its special events in such publications may be the easiest and most effective way of getting the message your targeted audience. However, the museum must provide accurate and detailed information in the prescribed form in time to meet publication deadlines. For example, the deadline for the Wisconsin spring/summer calendar of events falls in early September, six months before its projected mailing and nine months before the beginning of the next summer's tourist season. Museums desiring to capitalize on this free publicity should schedule dates and hours of operations and major events almost a year in advance in order to meet these strict deadlines.

The Wisconsin Department of Tourism promotional effort includes a cooperative advertising program, which gives reduced rates for participants that advertise with other attractions. The department also develops its own ads for television, radio, and newspapers. Museums could contact the department about highlighting their events in these ads.

The department contracted with a public relations firm to provide public relations services. The firm sends seasonal kits with articles and facts about Wisconsin tourism to media outlets nationwide. It sends out news releases, handles travel media in-

quiries, and surveys tourism organizations each season to identify interesting events and attractions. Wisconsin museums desiring to increase visitorship would benefit by making sure they
are on the firm's mailing list. The firm also publishes free
newsletters on marketing for the state's tourism community.
One issue addressed how to write press releases, feature stories, cover letters, and photo captions. Another discussed developing an effective media kit. The department provides these
newsletters free of charge.

If your state tourism or economic development offices do not
provide these types of services, investigate statewide organizations, chambers of commerce, or convention bureaus. A few
telephone calls may provide free or low-cost market data, lists
of media contacts with addresses and telephone numbers, and
other material useful to a museum.

After you have identified potential resources, work with them
to develop an appropriate media marketing program. This requires at least four steps. First, create a list of the media likely
to reach the target market effectively. Second, develop appropriate press releases and media kits. The Biltmore Estate,
Asheville, N.C., for example, developed an elaborate media kit
that included a book detailing the history of the house, press
releases on different aspects of programs and the maintenance
of the mansion, a schedule of events, and excellent, 8-by-10-
inch black-and-white photographs. Third, make follow-up
phone calls to your media contacts. Fourth, arrange on-site
tours for journalists, which the tourist industry calls familiarization or FAM tours. Debbie Geiger, an expert in heritage
tourism marketing, says that the feature stories that influence
travel decisions almost always come from journalists who have
actually visited the site (Geiger 1991, 6-11).

A museum should try to obtain free coverage from publications or other media used by the target audience. Free cover-

age not only fits your budget, but is more influential than paid advertising. According to Geiger, a number of major research studies indicate that word-of-mouth recommendations and editorial stories have the most influence on people's travel decisions. Do not underestimate the actual dollar value of free coverage. Compare the columns of press generated by public relations efforts with the cost of that space in paid advertising.

Elizabeth Sims, the Biltmore Estate's public relations manager, says that "the most effective part of public relations is through generating news stories." Sims finds that the public has appreciated articles about how staff clean the 19th-century house, make Christmas decorations, care for the silver, and restore 16th-century tapestries.

To obtain free coverage, a museum must develop and sustain positive media contacts over a period of time. You can do this by developing a talent for determining what stories the media will deem newsworthy, having accurate and complete facts, and providing useful information to the right media contact in a timely manner. Do not, for example, call newspaper reporters about a Christmas tour hours before deadline. Do not provide magazines with information about your Fourth of July event in June, as their summer issues have already gone to the printer. Do not send photographs of poor quality or without signed releases from each person pictured.

If the museum director, staff, or key volunteers do not have public relations expertise, talk to local business people who do. Invite the local newspaper editor to lunch at the museum restaurant or another nearby establishment. Talk to the public relations director at the local college as well as to faculty members who teach the subject. Get the reading list, go to the bookstore, and browse through the recommended reading. Fairly simple lists of standard "do's and don'ts" exist. Marketing is not rocket science, but it does require definition, diligence, imagination, and common sense.

Be clear and be consistent. Create a single symbol for the museum that conveys the desired message, and use only that symbol in all promotion efforts. Businesses do this. How many Americans do not know the significance of the McDonald's golden arches? Develop a phrase (slogan) that captures the essence of the visitor experience at your museum, and use it again and again. An advertising agency providing help to the Cheney Cowles Museum, in Spokane, Wash., created the slogan "Dutch Treat" for a special exhibit of old masters from the Netherlands. The phrase, which was used in all the museum's publicity, helped attract a record audience.

Once the museum leadership approves a market plan, it should maintain it for a reasonable length of time. Results will not be immediate. Levinson recommends approaching the plan as a long-term investment that requires commitment before results occur. Another expert, Peggy Bendel, formerly with Development Counselors International, New York, says that a museum sometimes decides that its message is stale exactly at the time that it has become effective.

Museums should partner with other institutions to maximize their public relations efforts. The Indianapolis Symphony uses the grounds of Conner Prairie, Fishers, Ind., for summer evening performances. The museum has increased both visitation and gift shop sales due to the crowds attending the symphony. More important, Conner Prairie receives free, summer-long publicity throughout the Indianapolis market area. Chapter 5 includes more examples of partnerships that provide public relations and other benefits.

Successful marketing requires a commitment of time, energy, and money. Often, you can find ways to cut costs and use donated services. But outstanding marketing efforts require intent, dedication of resources, and professional knowledge and experience. Jan Wigen, development officer at the Cheney

Cowles Museum, mounted the outstanding campaign that attracted visitors to the exhibit of Dutch and Flemish masters. The effort won a media award for excellence from the American Association of Museums. Wigen had private-sector marketing experience and was able to persuade a large advertising agency to donate its services. Still, she had to push aside all regular work for months to accomplish the task. Much of the campaign's success lay in innovative public relations, which started with the creation of the exhibition's catchy slogan, "Dutch Treat." However, not everyone was pleased with the slogan; there were some museum staff who preferred the phrase "Dutch Masters."

Many museums may not be able to undertake all of Wigen's steps and activities. However, all museums will gain some tips from this outstanding museum marketing effort.

References

1994 Market Report. Washington, D.C.: U.S. Travel Data Center, Travel Industry Association, 1995.

Geiger, Debbie. "Generating Media Coverage of History Sites," *Historic Preservation Forum* (July/August 1991): 6-11.

In-flight Survey of International Travelers: Profile of Overseas Travelers to U.S. Destinations, January-December, 1994. Washington, D.C.: U.S. Travel and Tourism Administration, 1995.

Ketterer, James P. *International Tourism: New York's Opportunity for the '90s.* Albany, N.Y.: Senate Committee on Tourism, Recreation and Sports Development, 1990.

Levinson, Jay Conrad. *Guerrilla Marketing.* Boston: Houghton Mifflin Company, 1993.

Lord Cultural Resources Planning & Management Inc. *The Cultural Tourism Handbook.* Toronto, Canada: Lord Cultural Resources Planning & Management Inc., 1993.

Mature America in the 1990s: A Special Report from Modern Maturity

Magazine and the Roper Organization. Washington, D.C.: American Association of Retired Persons, 1992.

Receipts and Payments Trend Analysis: 1986-1996, rev. Washington, D.C.: U.S. Travel and Tourism Administration, Office of Research, Bureau of Economic Analysis, 1995.

Regionalizing VALS Research: Final Report. Madison, Wis.: State of Wisconsin Department of Tourism, 1995.

Silberberg, Ted. "The Importance of Market and Feasibility Analysis" in *The Manual of Museum Planning,* ed. Gail Dexter and Barry Lord. London: HMSO Publications Centre, 1991, 53-70.

Tourism Works for America 1996 Report. Washington, D.C.: Tourism Works for America Council, 1996.

Waters, Somerset. *Travel Industry World Yearbook.* Washington, D.C.: U.S. Travel Data Center, 1992.

Partnerships

Museums can increase their economic potential by forming partnerships. Many types of organizations make good partners, including local civic groups, economic development organizations, consortia, other nonprofit organizations, private businesses, and schools.

I. Possible Partners

A. Other museums

Smaller museums often do not have the money to produce professional quality brochures. Five museums on the southwest coast of Washington State collaborated on a joint brochure called "Rain or Shine: Explore the Museums and Centers of Pacific County, Washington." By pooling their funds and ideas, they produced 3,000 copies of an attractive two-color brochure. Working alone, the museums could not have afforded a two-color publication or as many copies. They also saved money on postage and labor since each museum's outreach programs benefited them all. By the time the brochure needed reprinting, several other area museums wanted to participate, providing further savings and cross-marketing opportunities.

B. Partnerships with local civic groups

The SS Meteor Museum in Superior, Wis., is located in the world's only remaining whaleback freighter. Local and tourist visitation, however, did not generate sufficient operating revenue until the museum collaborated with the local junior chamber of commerce on an annual 14-day haunted house tour. The ship and its dock provide an ideal setting, according to organizer David Miner: "It's dark, cold, windy. It squeaks. It makes noise all by itself. We don't have to add a lot of special effects to make it work."

The junior chamber of commerce provides 72 volunteers for each evening tour and the two matinees. Museum staff maintain the ship, create the marketing promotions, and build the props. Local merchants, individuals, and the media donate services and materials, or offer reduced rates. The museum and the junior chamber of commerce split the profits. Through this event, the museum not only generates revenue, but also builds solid community links.

C. Partnerships with economic development organizations

A project sponsored by the State Historical Society of Wisconsin to explore the potential for involving museums in regional economic development efforts initially encountered several stumbling blocks. Originally, the organizers planned to interview museum directors and economic development planners, and then host a conference focusing on the potential of museum and economic development partnerships. Unfortunately, all the interviewees declined to attend. The museum directors said that they would allocate their limited travel funds to attending the annual Wisconsin Federation of Museums meeting. The economic development practitioners simply shrugged, saying, "*What?* Museums?"

It was obvious that the museums and economic development practitioners did not talk to each other. Members of the chambers of commerce and other economic developers complained that the museum directors did not understand tourism needs and did not participate in community efforts. Museum directors complained that they attracted tourists but did not receive any recognition.

The project had to change to succeed. With funds from the project's budget, the organizers invited 15 leaders to a roundtable discussion at a resort near a historic house. At first, the discussion centered on people's complaints, and there was little identification of any mutual cooperative efforts. A suggestion that museums interpret the region's 300-year history and market themselves together in a single package elicited no agreement. Finally, an hour before the end of the roundtable, one museum director said that he would not object to featuring his museum on a poster-style map with other museums, and the group decided to proceed with that project. The participants also agreed that the roundtable was in fact valuable; people made contacts and started relationships. They asked for additional dialogue.

An *ad hoc* committee of museums and economic developers was formed to establish criteria and guide the development of the map project. Initially expected to feature between 15 and 25 museums, the final map covered a 12-county region and had information on about 38 museums. The printing of the map was paid for by a grant from the International Business and Economic Development Council (ITBEC), an organization of the 12 counties. ITBEC also funded a public relations campaign for the map.

Museum staff began attending workshops on economic development. The president of the Wisconsin Federation of Museums considered establishing a subcommittee for the area covered by the map. Museum directors began to talk to each other and to economic developers. The State Department of Tourism and Heritage Tourism Program sponsored a workshop that taught museum directors more about marketing, and encouraged them to develop joint efforts in the future. A regional approach to marketing had begun.

What made it work? The prestige and personal reputation of H. Nicholas Muller, III, then director of the State Historical Society of Wisconsin, encouraged people to participate in the initial interviews. He also provided credibility for the roundtable. The organizers telephoned the roundtable participants several times to encourage attendance. The resort provided an elegant setting for the meeting. The schedule enabled directors to leave their offices late one day and, if necessary, return the next. Outside funding meant that the roundtable and the project could proceed without any initial financial investment by the museums or economic developers.

D. Partnerships with regional organizations

Generally, effective community economic and tourism development succeeds when community organizations cooperate. Extensive tourism development requires infrastructure such as parking, as well as long-range planning and the support of various groups such as taxpayers. Museums can maximize their economic development efforts by joining such efforts. The investment also will build community goodwill and create an understanding of the museum's contributions among government and business leaders. In some cases, the job of serving on appropriate chamber of commerce committees or the tourism board can be delegated to a museum board member or volunteer.

The National Trust for Historic Preservation's Main Street program has helped revitalize hundreds of small towns throughout America, employing historic preservation as a key component in economic development and downtown revitalization. The program emphasizes cooperation among a broad-based coalition of merchants, public officials, and civic groups, which then can develop approaches for improving the visual quality of downtown areas, strengthening and diversifying the economic base.

Wisconsin's Chippewa Valley Museum played a major role in a multi-phased program. The museum helped to produce a self-guided history walking tour of the downtown area for the Eau Claire Main Street program by providing research and photographic materials. "Unlike most walking tours that stress architecture," says Jim Schuh, former executive director of Eau Claire Main Street, the guide described the history of the community and the role that downtown businesses played in its development. Museum staff also helped identify historic sites and properties and provided information and photographs for a directory called *Timber Trails in the Chippewa Valley*, which identified heritage attractions tied to the area's lumber industry. Schuh gives most of the credit for the overall success of the effort to Susan McLeod, the museum's director, who chaired the Momentum Chippewa Valley Tourism Development Committee. According to Schuh, McLeod persuaded organizations in three counties to develop the joint project, which eventually received funding from the Wisconsin Heritage Tourism Program and local contributors.

The Southwestern Pennsylvania Heritage Preservation Commission (SPHPC) is another powerful example of how a partnership can lead to results far beyond the resources of individual museums or communities. In 1988, Congress established the commission to preserve, promote, and interpret the industrial and cultural heritage in a nine-county area. The commission is a partnership among federal, state, county, and local

units of government; the private sector; and community and
heritage organizations. It interprets the history of the region's
natural resources and their extraction, industrial and technological development, and the changing patterns of immigra-
tion. The commission identified three heritage corridors that
best illustrate this history, each one highlighting different historic and scenic sites and resources. It promotes the area
through interpretative materials, displays, and highway signs
that identify the 500-mile-long heritage route. It has established standards for inclusion that address a site's relevance to
the overall story, the adequacy of its facilities, as well as its
preservation standards.

In addition, the commission encourages counties to develop related heritage routes as side tours. Each of the nine counties
has produced brochures that identify heritage resources of local or regional interest. For example, the Indiana County
brochure highlights Blairsville, a town that was founded in
1818 and contains a number of historic buildings. The
brochure recommends a visit to "the museum operated by the
Historical Society of the Blairsville area . . . to travel back to
those significant days of our transportation heritage." It also
describes other sites of potential interest to tourists, including
several parks and recreation areas.

Museums and historical societies play a major role in the commission's effort. Members of the Pennsylvania Historical and
Museum Commission, the Pennsylvania Heritage Affairs Commission, and county heritage committees also serve as members
of SPHPC. Museums such as the Altoona Railroader's Memor-
ial Museum and the Johnstown Flood Museum rank high
among the corridor attractions.

Approximately 125 other regions in the country have begun to
develop heritage corridors. Some have built new interpretative
centers, such as the gigantic End of the Trail covered wagon

center in Oregon City, Oreg. These efforts can provide museums with increased publicity and visitors. Museums desiring inclusion in multi-site projects should get involved as early as possible. For example, a number of museums in southwest Washington had only a vague awareness that there was a plan to promote attractions located near a major highway in the area. Had they communicated with economic and tourism developers, they could have participated in and helped to shape the planning.

Sometimes a planning organization or a town chooses to create its own museum or interpretative center rather than expand or modify an existing one. This can dilute the curatorial and research resources of existing museums, especially if the interpretative centers rely on multimedia exhibits that do not require careful restoration and preservation. In addition, these institutions often do not budget for exhibit upgrades or replacements.

The proliferation of museums in an area can inundate the market unless each institution provides a different approach to the overall story. To resolve this issue, the Oregon Trail Coordinating Council helped museums and interpretative centers develop different emphases, while sharing resources and marketing. An interpretative center at Flagstaff Hill, Oreg., located near Baker City in the eastern part of the state, provides visitors with an opportunity to walk beside Oregon Trail ruts and view the Powder River Valley, which is described in pioneers' diaries as the first point of fulfillment of their Oregon Territory dream. On the other side of the state is the End of the Trail Interpretative Center, constructed as three giant covered wagons. There, visitors can see what 19th-century travelers packed into their wagons, as well as learn about the early settlement of the region. The Tamustalik Interpretive Institute on the Umatilla Indian Reservation presents the history, culture, and tradition of local native groups, the impact of Euro-American contact on the indigenous people, and shows how traditional tribal values affect contemporary life. The Columbia Gorge Discovery Center at The Dalles in Stevenson, Wash., focuses on the critical decision made by settlers at that point: whether to cross the dangerous Columbia River on rafts or climb the tall mountain. Visitors can enjoy any of these interpretative centers separately, but find fresh presentations and insights when they visit them all.

E. Partnerships with other cultural organizations

Years ago, Conner Prairie, Fishers, Ind., a living history village and museum near Indianapolis, teamed up with the Indianapolis Symphony Orchestra for a summer outdoor symphony series called "Marsh Symphony on the Prairie." Since then, a sophisticated partnership has developed. Conner Prairie provides a lovely outdoor space with parking, restrooms, and a band shell. The symphony provides the musical programs and publicity, buying radio and newspaper advertising during the eight-week concert session. Symphony staff mail brochures to both institutions' mailing lists, as well as place brochures in racks throughout the city and insert them in an alternative newspaper with a circulation of 40,000. The museum's logo, along with the special logo for the concert series, is featured on the brochure, which invites people to visit the museum before the concert begins.

Although only one-fourth of those attending the concerts first visit the museum, the Marsh Symphony on the Prairie promotions heighten community awareness of the museum throughout the summer. The museum also benefits from the rental fees, increased shop sales, and revenue from the concessions stands, which serve picnic dinners and snacks. The symphony benefits from the lovely outdoor setting, a facility with ample parking and restroom facilities, and a larger audience. The symphony's indoor facility holds 1,800 people. But at Conner Prairie, they have played to crowds numbering 15,000. The concert series "is a money maker for us [that] easily doubles normal winter attendance at each performance," says symphony marketer Rachel Riegel.

Conner Prairie and the symphony work closely together to prepare the appropriate facilities and marketing arrangements, and have developed a contract that details their respective responsibilities. Your museum may not have the space for a large musical event, but perhaps it could host a quartet or other smaller ensemble.

F. Partnerships with the private sector

The Denver Children's Museum has undertaken a number of highly successful ventures in cooperation with the private sector. For example, they contracted with Citicorp to produce a book on money and the economy, which the bank could give to its customers. Citicorp carefully reviewed the text, forcing museum staff to re-examine interpretations and presentations. The debates resulted in a missed deadline, but led to a product that effectively presented more complex economic issues to children than the museum staff had believed possible (Steckel 1989, 41).

G. Partnerships with charitable organizations

The Mint Museum of Art in Charlotte, N.C., houses an internationally recognized porcelain collection. Staff worried that "Service in Style: Regal Soup Tureens," a traveling exhibition organized in 1992 by the Campbell Museum, Camden, N.J., would have limited attendance and "reinforce a public stereotype of museums being a high-brow sanctuary of the wealthy," says Phil Busher, public relations coordinator. They paraphrased Marie Antoinette's famous remark, turning it into "let them eat soup," and mounted a major campaign that focused attention on the needs of homeless and hungry people in the area.

The museum offered free admission from Nov. 1 through Thanksgiving to anyone who brought a can of food for the Metrolina Food Bank. Publicity for the event incorporated the Mint's well-known painting of the coronation of Queen Charlotte—with a Campbell's tomato soup can substituted for the coronation crown. The *Leader* newspaper, local radio station WEZC, and Price Waterhouse provided sponsorship. Flyers were sent to 6,000 churches and press releases to 463 media outlets asking them to publicize the event. The results? Twice as much media coverage of the museum, a record-setting 21,426 visitors during the six-week exhibit, and 5,000 pounds of food donated to the food bank.

H. Partnership with neighborhood groups

The Chicago Historical Society has begun a multi-year collaboration with four neighborhoods. The society's collection contains photographs and other materials that reflect the history and variety of Chicago's neighborhoods. The collaboration reflects board's desire for increased outreach and greater emphasis on the city's diverse ethnic history.

The project started with the Douglas/Grand Boulevard area on the south side. Formerly called Bronzeville, the area served as a center of African-American life through the 1940s. The project director, who had previously worked with community organizations, created a committee of neighborhood residents and groups to collaborate with the society's educational and curatorial staff. Working together, they produced an exhibit that was displayed first at the society and then at the DuSable Museum of African American History, which is located near the neighborhood. The exhibit included items found in residents' attics as well as a video presentation produced by local teen-agers.

As part of the overall project, one group interviewed young and elderly residents for a neighborhood oral history project. Another group worked with local teachers to develop related curriculum materials for the schools. Educational and cultural events, such as films, lectures and performances, were presented in schools and other neighborhood facilities during the year-long effort.

Related programs at the DuSable Museum included a symposium on economic and social life during the Bronzeville era; a three-part discussion on the literary works and writers, such as Richard Wright, connected with the area; a movie series; jazz, blues, and gospel concerts; and a series of genealogy workshops. The community's pride in the exhibit was demonstrated by positive comments from a museum volunteer, the museum guard, and workmen who were involved in its installation.

II. Benefits and Risks of Partnerships

These are examples of some of the potential partners for museums. The goals of a specific partnership will vary, but they might include enhancing your exhibits, gaining additional expertise, or collaborating on public relations or marketing efforts, fund raising, or programming. The benefits can be enormous. What are the risks?

A partnership should support the museum's major mission. For example, I had a discussion about increasing attendance with the director of a university museum, who emphasized that the museum's mission was to serve the university community. The director wanted to attract repeat visitors from the university and local artists who might develop a close relationship with staff. For that museum, a partnership with an organization promoting tourism would be inappropriate.

Even an appropriate partnership may not prove wise if it takes away attention from more important objectives. The Denver

Children's Museum produced a children's exhibit for a sheep producers association that included activities dealing with sheep shearing and the process of turning raw wool into fabric. Although children liked the show, staff questioned whether it had kept them from producing other exhibits that were more educationally valuable (Steckel 1989, 42).

Staff at the museum also were concerned about promoting products incompatible with the best interests of children, a problem that arose when a soft drink manufacturer wanted to advertise in a museum-produced school newspaper. And they were concerned about maintaining control over exhibit and product content during the production of the Citicorp publication. Museum partnerships, like any others, will thrive when they rest solidly on objectives that meet the needs of both partners. Partnerships should draw upon the special abilities of each organization, and participants should have a clear understanding of objectives, tasks, roles, responsibilities, benefits, and the terms for potential dissolution. Putting these factors in writing clarifies issues and can help to resolve problems before they become sources of friction.

References

Steckel, Dr. Richard, Robin Simons, and Peter Lengsfelder. *Filthy Rich and Other Nonprofit Fantasies: Changing the way nonprofits do business in the '90s.* Berkeley, Calif.: Ten Speed Press, 1989.

6 Events and Festivals

Community events and festivals further both a museum's mission and the area's economic development. They attract tourists and almost always make the community a more attractive place to live, adding to the community's ability to retain businesses and attract new ones. They build community pride and provide opportunities for community members to enhance their skills and meet people who may not move in their social circles. Newcomers will welcome such opportunities.

Events and festivals can serve as some of a museum's most effective fund-raising strategies by generating both direct profits and indirect support. They can assist a museum promoting memberships, donations, and planned giving, increasing publicity and attendance, and encouraging greater commitment from volunteers. Studies indicate that contributions to charitable organizations from volunteers more than double contributions from non-volunteers. Major donations and planned giving, including bequests from wills, life insurance and annuities, pooled income funds and various kinds of trusts, almost always come from members or donors who have contributed regularly for three or more years. Events should broaden the base of a museum's support.

But these efforts also can backfire, resulting in adverse publicity, angry volunteers, and exhausted staff. One cynic familiar with nonprofit organizations quipped that "a successful fundraiser is one who doesn't lose money." In fact, when determining whether your event will break even, take into account non-cash assets such as staff time, goodwill, and other resources that might have been employed more profitably. Since a particular festival or event often loses momentum after three or five years, when volunteer and public interest decreases, museums need to track results carefully and switch to an alternative event at the appropriate time. The bibliography includes fund-raising books with sections on events, as well as information on membership and other fund-raising possibilities.

Museum staff can participate in a variety of ways, from serving on a planning committee to helping to publicize a community-wide event to operating a large festival. Determining the appropriate level of involvement requires a cost-benefit analysis that examines mission, financial rewards, and community relations.

I. Renting Museum Facilities or Grounds

Most museums embody elements of elegance and prestige. They provide a special ambience for a wedding, corporate board dinner, or party. Museums and historic homes have provided locations for symphony and chamber music concerts, regional art shows, and photographing commercial models and movies. Whether renting proves appropriate or profitable for a particular museum depends upon a number of factors.

You can avoid several problems by developing a written rental policy. Staff, key volunteers, and the museum's lawyer and insurance agent should review it before it is adopted. Contracts should contain provisions for cancellations and for the resolution of problems and disagreements.

A. Developing a rental policy

1. Preservation of structure, objects, and grounds

The Hermann-Grima Historic House, New Orleans, hosts receptions on its grounds, but restricts the location, size, and frequency to avoid damage to the lawn and other facility problems. The Philadelphia Museum of Art provides space for entertainment events of nonprofit groups and members of its Corporate Partners program, but prohibits food and drink in areas where art is on display. Wade House, Greenbush, Wis., had to line its cookstove's chimney after staff began hosting dinners cooked over the open hearth by guests.

2. Compatibility with museum mission and image

Hosting a major Civil War re-enactment makes sense for Wade House, which served as a recruitment center during the Civil War. The same event, however, would appear out-of-place in an urban art museum. If a museum's marketing plan conveys one image while its special events suggest another, target audiences may find the mixed message confusing. But this is less likely if the museum is not sponsoring an event but only renting its space to another organization. Still, some restrictions are needed.

3. Compatibility with existing programs and facilities

Is participating in this event the best way to use staff time? Will the event detract from regular programs or turn away loyal visitors? Will it require modifications such as more parking spaces, additional dishes, or new plants? Who pays for these changes? Does the event disrupt regular museum activities? Biltmore Estate in Asheville, N.C., rents its facility for movies, but tries to schedule shootings during its slow season, since film-making requires re-arranging rooms and disrupts normal tours.

4. Legal, personnel, and insurance considerations
What are the zoning requirements? Do you need a special permit? What kind of liquor can be served? Should you get a liquor license? Your insurance agent may recommend that the museum or its clients obtain additional coverage. If additional guards are required, who will hire, supervise, and pay them? What if the renter wants to sell or auction items, as might occur at an annual fund-raising charity ball?

After considering all these items, a museum may want to limit the types of events, as well as their size and timing, or enforce other restrictions. The fee schedule should reflect direct and indirect costs and provide funds as a reserve for the depreciation of plant and equipment.

A properly designed rental policy will enable museums to preserve their missions, objects, grounds, and images. Such a policy also helps you to balance demands on staff and volunteers with the needs of regular visitors and programs.

Finally, each museum must determine the role it will play during the events. Some museums simply lease their facilities. Others cater events or arrange for catering. Still others arrange the entire event for the renter. During an exhibition of Dutch masters at the Cheney Cowles Museum, Spokane, Wash., local businesses were invited to host private corporate evenings at the museum. The proposal letter sent to the companies included the following lists of responsibilities:

Museum's Responsibilities:
 museum facility rental
 free admission for event guests to the "A Sumptuous Past"
  exhibition

receptionist during event hours
security guard during event hours
professional staff person during event hours
trained docents during event hours
museum custodian during event hours
visitor orientation
tables (up to eight 6-foot rectangular tables and two six-
    seater round tops)
chairs (up to 45 folding chairs)
supervision of and assistance to caterer for event
free access to Dutch Hypoteek Bank exhibition
free access to exhibition of museum's collection of
    Dutch masters

Businesses' Responsibilities:
obtain banquet permit under business name
arrange and pay for all catering
rent additional furniture, if necessary
add museum to company insurance policy for event period

The museum also developed facility rental regulations and a fa-
cilities-use contract for the events.

II. Sponsoring Events, Festivals, and Products

Museums raise funds by sponsoring or co-sponsoring a wide
variety of events, limited only by imagination and resources.
The small Swedish-American Museum in Swedesburg, Iowa, a
village of less than 100 people, raises money by selling traditional Swedish cookies and coffee during museum tours and
providing traditional Swedish meals for bus tour visitors. The
Philbrook Museum of Art, Tulsa, Okla., taps more extensive
resources for its annual fall gala. The formal black tie dinner
dance for more than 400 people includes a silent auction that
offers items not available on the open market, such as a week
on a private yacht or a ski vacation at a private home in Aspen,
Colo.

Museum-sponsored events have included lectures, field trips to local and foreign places, concerts, and historic re-enactments. Product development ranges from reproductions of museum pieces to T-shirts, from dolls to educational games. Items vary with the museum's mission, collection, staff, and other resources.

A. Know the market

Director Edgar Oerichbauer says that his institution, Forts Folle Avoine, Siren, Wis., has held the only museum-sponsored ice fishing contest. "People here won't pay $25 to come to a dinner . . . but we made an average of $7,000 to $10,000 from our annual ice fishing contest," he says. For 12 years, several thousand people went to the museum to try their luck at catching a tagged fish or to watch others fish. The event ended after insurance became a problem and the state banned tagged-fish contests.

B. Use the museum's uniqueness

Wade House boasts a working open hearth kitchen, has original owner Betsey Wade's cookbooks, and has a staff member with a degree in folk studies and an interest in historical food preparation methods. Deciding to "play to our strengths," the museum hosts Yankee Harvest Dinners, says the director. Guests spend the day cooking historically traditional dishes in a traditional manner, while costumed staff provide explanations, guidance, and copies of the recipes. People gladly pay $30 each to attend. Many come every year, some in costume. The SS Meteor Museum, Superior, Wis., provides another example. In late October, the museum capitalizes on its cold, dreary atmosphere to create a very profitable haunted house tour.

C. Support the vendors

In 1987, Wade House's arts-and-crafts fair attracted six vendors. By 1995, the event had become a juried event with 125 crafts persons presenting handmade crafts created in a traditional manner. It attracted 4,500 visitors in one day. The museum's director attributes the success to "treating the vendors very well. We spend a lot of money on postage and the telephone because we want . . . personal contact." The museum had to convince vendors that the Wade House event would merit their participation. Now, when the vendors arrive at 6 a.m., Curator Sally Wood greets each one individually. According to the director, "Sally is very careful to put them in the locations that they like." Before the event closes, she asks each vendor if they want the same spot for their booth the next year. "We always do written evaluations, even if it's just a page. What went well? What didn't go so well? What equipment is needed?"

Staff also tell the vendors how good they are. They provide a $30 cash award to the five best booths based on the attractiveness of their displays and how effectively the artists explained their craft. Polaroid pictures of the winners are posted on a bulletin board at the museum's entrance.

D. Relate events to the mission

Part of the mission of Conner Prairie, Fishers, Ind., is to teach 19th-century American history and keep traditional crafts alive. Its collection includes samples of needlework. When a local needlework store approached the museum's staff for assistance in sponsoring a workshop, they agreed. In its third year, the event attracted 2,000 persons in a four-day period, earning between $20,000 and $25,000 for the museum, primarily through sales in the restaurant and gift shops. The announcement for the event included lists of nearby attractions to visit, shops with related items for sale, hotels, and restaurants, thus providing assistance to local businesses.

E. Joint Venture

The "Wade House Civil War Re-enactment" takes place adjacent to Wade House, built in 1850 as a stage coach stop. The building also served as a recruiting station for Civil War enlistments. Original owners Sylvanus and Betsey Wade had three sons who fought in the war and three daughters who served as nurses. A recruiting effort in July 1861 featured a mock battle, not far from where the re-enactment battle occurs today. In 1995, Wade House's annual Civil War Weekend attracted almost 1,000 participants and about 10,000 visitors. The director credits the program's success to "some really good advice from some people who know what re-enactments are all about."

The museum relies upon help from more than 75 volunteers, local Civil War organizations, and 25 part-time and four full-time staff to produce the event. A group of Civil War "re-enactors," including a local historian who has published several books on the war, serve as an advisory committee for the event. Staff and committee members plan the mock battle, selecting an area with the most authentic topography; clear trees and brush; and assign spaces for campsites and horses. In order to interest re-enactors several years in a row, the committee alters the locations of the battle and campsites each year. Participants contribute hundreds of hours of volunteer time, pitching tents, bedding horses, and helping to clear the area where the battle is staged.

Local business and civic organizations, government, and individuals donate money and services for the event. In 1994, this amounted to $8,000 in cash and approximately $10,000 in free advertisements and donated food and equipment. The Civil War Weekend gives visitors an opportunity to talk to "925 intensely motivated people wanting to share history," says the director. "I defy anyone to come to this event and not learn some history." It also makes money for the museum. In 1994, it

grossed $67,000 (including donated cash) with a net profit of
more than $30,000.

The enormous logistics include arranging for $1,100 of black
gunpowder, water and straw for 50 to 60 horses, a hospital tent
for emergency medical services, toilets, parking, and rations
(each participant receives cabbage, carrots, coffee, and sugar,
typical fare for a Civil War soldier). The re-enactors, like all
armies, "travel on their stomachs," says the director. To manage this complex event, the director keeps detailed records on
four computers.

According to the director, basic customer service is what
makes this joint venture work. Continued success depends
upon delivering what you promised, providing courteous treat-
ment, and paying attention to logistical details. Without a
strong program, the event would lose momentum, he says. "Big
events will disappear in two years because you didn't take care
of something as seemingly trivial as the firewood." Staff also
spend much of their time seeking good commanders for the re-
enactment units and taking care of the participants: "We really
go out of our way to make them happy [and] they really appreciate it. . . ," says the director.

F. Sell products to business

In recent years, the Denver Children's Museum has developed
a number of successful entrepreneurial ventures. Staff began
these efforts by analyzing their mission and identifying the services and products that they had an unique ability to provide.
The first project, a specially designed traveling exhibit called
"Sensorium," gave children the opportunity to participate in
music, drama, art, and dance activities. The rental cost for
"Sensorium" was $1,500 for a four-day period; the exhibit was
marketed primarily to shopping malls anxious to attract families. In three years, "Sensorium" netted the museum $25,000.

The museum then published several books as corporate premium items, gifts offered by businesses to attract customers. These included *A-Maze-ing Denver,* a children's game incorporating Denver landmarks, which was sold to a real estate firm; *The Babysitter's Guide,* sold to a chain of day care centers, a bank, and a home builder; and *The Frontier Flying Fun Book,* which was sold to Frontier Airlines. Museum staff also created a children's newspaper, which they gave to elementary schools throughout the Denver area, creating a circulation of 100,000 that attracted advertisers. At one point, the newspaper netted $18,000 a year for the museum.

Richard Steckel, former executive director of the Denver Children's Museum, suggests adopting the following principles:

1. Obtain seed funds for production costs from a corporate marketing partner.

2. Sell the product wholesale to a corporation, which will then distribute it to individuals.

3. Determine an accurate pricing structure that includes direct development costs, indirect costs (staff time, overhead), and profit.

4. Maintain quality control. The museum's reputation as an expert in family education requires control over quality and content.

5. Diversify. Provide a variety of products in case one does not succeed.
(Steckel 1989, 38-39)

Just as important, the products must reflect the museum's mission, and the museum's organizational climate and staff must encourage entrepreneurial approaches. A product also should meet a specific need of the targeted corporation (Steckel 1989, 39). The Denver Children's Museum saw its mission not just as supporting children's education in a narrow sense but also as developing positive self-images. Printing *The Babysitter's Guide* enabled the museum to share its expertise about activities that promote positive interactions between child and adult. And by distributing the publication through other organizations and businesses, the museum was able to reach a much broader audience.

A museum should select its entrepreneurial activities carefully. Museums often face moral or ethical dilemmas about which products and sponsors are appropriate. Entrepreneurship may only be appropriate for certain products, at a specific point in a museum's development, for some museums, or under certain leadership. For example, after Steckel left the Denver Children's Museum, the museum shifted priorities and decreased its entrepreneurial efforts.

G. Use the marketing systems of other groups

A number of museums have begun offering Elderhostel programs, which offer educational and travel experiences for persons ages 55 and over and their companions. A museum serving as an Elderhostel site provides 22-1/2 hours of instruction, arranges for local lodging and meals, organizes evening and other entertainment and provides an on-site coordinator during the week. Museums often find that they gain increased publicity and community goodwill. Local media usually consider field trips and other Elderhostel activities good material for feature stories.

By participating, museums can gain access to a national market almost ideal for their potential programs. The Elderhostel organization sends its program announcement to more than 800,000 persons quarterly, about half of whom participate in the program. They are typically retired professionals and their spouses who travel, listen to public radio and watch public television, particularly programs on art and history. A high percentage of people who participate in one Elderhostel program re-enroll. Multi-generational programs also are becoming popular with grandparents and grandchildren.

H. Calculate costs, benefits, and risks carefully, and keep accurate records

The success of all potential fund-raising activities depends on the museum. Whether the Elderhostel program is appropriate for a particular institution, and whether it will need subsidies, break even, or prove profitable, depends upon the museum's mission, staff, and the way the program is operated. Conduct careful calculations and maintain accurate tracking of costs and income to determine the financial consequences of the program operation.

The Witte Museum, San Antonio, Tex., has hosted Elderhostel programs for six years. During the first five years, the program did not make money, although it did help pay the salaries of two staff members. During this period, however, citing the large number of program participants provided credibility to the Witte's applications for grants for educational diversity. In the long-run, other benefits might occur. For example, a participant might become a donor or leave the museum a bequest. In 1996, the Witte ran 21 Elderhostel programs, which served 1,000 people, and finally turned a profit.

The Chicago Historical Society operates several Elderhostel programs a year, but only breaks even, and these calculations do not include the costs of staff time. This does not worry staff, however, because the program provides effective outreach to an audience their mission requires them to serve. On the other hand, Conner Prairie, Fishers, Ind., decided that the effort to continue hosting a needlework workshop weekend required a larger investment of staff time than could be justified, given the final profits. Staff modified their approach, developing a smaller, more cost-effective event. And Public Affairs Director

Brenda Myers warns that such programs can affect a museum's attendance figures, as people may start visiting only during the special event times.

Mark Lane, former director of the Witte Museum, cautions museums to carefully research all the critical factors before adopting a fund-raising project or event. He strongly urges considering the "downside" or possible losses, and balancing them with the potential "upside." Since most events have significant start-up costs, the greatest benefits come from projects that can be repeated, with each event building on the expertise gained from the previous one, as well as those that re-use contacts, equipment, volunteers, and rekindle the good will generated by the previous year's event. Special programs, like product development, can serve a variety of purposes. Each museum must determine which events best optimize its mission, increase its target audience, and support its financial goals.

References

Steckel, Dr. Richard. *Filthy Rich and Other Nonprofit Fantasies: Changing the way nonprofits do business in the 90s.* Berkeley, Calif.: Ten Speed Press, Berkeley, 1989.

7 Conclusions

This book provides strategies that will help museums connect with their local economic development planners. When considering these suggestions, each museum should take into account its location, collection, mission, and vision. Economic development practitioners who want their local museums to contribute to the community's economic well-being should not only consider the benefits, but also each institution's mission and potential restrictions.

The book points out the immense potential of tourism as an economic development force. Both the current interest in cultural and historic tourism and the aging of the American population position museums to share in tourism's growth. Any museum considering tapping this market should weigh the pros and cons, and consider its own institutional constraints and opportunities. Chapter 2 provides some approaches for framing those decisions.

Several of the examples listed in this book simply reflect good visitor service, attractive exhibits, convenient hours, obtaining feedback from customers, and other aspects of sensitive management. Many museums of all sizes already reflect appropriate product development.

But on the whole, museums, especially small ones, do not actively market their attractions. To compete successfully in the leisure market, museums must master marketing skills and invest resources in public relations. Some inexpensive methods exist—private experts and agencies sometimes donate services, and partnerships can prove lucrative. At this time of reduced federal, state, and local funding, partnerships can maximize resources and may help institutions obtain government and corporate funding.

Special events, whether sponsored alone or in partnership, increase visibility and revenue. Earned income of all kinds helps museums to survive and convinces funders, local businesses, and others that museums understand "the bottom line," and can make business-like decisions. Events also can help boost the local economy.

Earning income and gaining community support by contributing to the local economy will not solve all of a museum's problems. In some cases, a partnership with an economic developer will increase complications and risk. One major risk is a growing desire by other groups to control the content of the museum's messages. If museums can build endowments or earn their own income, they become less vulnerable to outside pressure.

A museum's ability to deal responsibly with changing financial and social trends requires realistic assessment of challenges and opportunities. As museums reviewing their own role in economic development consider the points and examples listed in this book, they should ponder these larger issues and collectively develop a thoughtful and effective response.

Bibliography

This bibliography is for museum staff unfamiliar with some of the topics in this book. The publications listed range from basic presentations of a subject to approaches or insights unlikely to be gleaned from regular museum channels. Economic development practitioners will find information about basic museum operations as well as specific references on tourism and festivals. The annotations indicate each publication's contents as well as the target audience. For example, some will contain details of interest only to an event chair while others on the same subject will be more appropriate for a committee member or museum trustee. Still others provide background information on tourism, useful for museum staff working with chambers of commerce.

Not every item will interest every museum professional or financial practitioner. For example, museums that host special events or partner with a chamber of commerce at festival time should review the items on festivals. Large institutions with several professional staff may not want to look at the items on museum displays, though such publications would be extremely useful to a small history museum attempting to become more of a tourist attraction.

Museums should be able to find at least one resource that will help them hold realistic discussions, make decisions, and take action. In some cases, several publications cover similar material, but one or another may be more appropriate for a particular museum or easier to locate. The bibliography could have included numerous other works, but a comprehensive listing seemed less practical than an accessible guide to a few relevant works. The categories should serve as a quick index, but since some publications contain data useful for several purposes, the reader may want to consult related categories or skim the entire bibliography. For example, the publication describing a focus group effort that is listed under "product development" also could have been placed under "marketing."

General

Any museum seeking excellence and growth would benefit from membership and participation in the relevant national, regional, and state organizations. The American Association of Museums (AAM) provides extensive assistance, including a large annual conference; sponsorship of regional and special interest committees; publications, including the bimonthly magazine *Museum News* with excellent articles; and a bookstore (and accompanying catalogue) of relevant publications. For information, contact: American Association of Museums, 1575 Eye Street N.W., Suite 400, Washington, DC 20005; 202/289-1818; fax 202/289-6578; http://www.aam-us.org.

The Texas Association of Museums (TAM) hosts an annual meeting that has excellent speakers. Smaller than the AAM meeting, it provides a less overwhelming atmosphere for newcomers, who often are paired with mentors. Contact: Texas Association of Museums, P.O. Box 13353, Austin, TX 78711; 512/328-6812.

Both TAM and AAM publish sourcebooks with summaries of many of the sessions at their annual conferences. The sourcebooks provide an overview of the current museum field as well as leads to those active in a particular area.

Museums also will want to contact their state and regional associations. The American Association for State and Local History (AASLH) caters to large and small history museums and historic sites, presents a major conference each fall, hosts workshops, publishes a magazine called *History News*, and maintains a useful library of technical leaflets. For information, contact: American Association for State and Local History, 530 Church St., Suite 600, Nashville, TN 37219; 615/255-9271; http://www.nashville.net/~aaslh. (Note: The AASLH books listed below are available from Sage Publications, 2455 Teller Rd., Thousand Oaks, CA 91320.)

Other relevant national associations include:

Association of Science-Technology Centers, Inc., 1025 Vermont Ave. N.W., Suite 500, Washington, DC 20005; 202/783-7200; http://www.astc.org/astc.

Association of Youth Museums, 1775 K St. N.W., Suite 595, Washington, DC 20006; 202/466-4144; e-mail: aymdc@aol.com.

National Trust for Historic Preservation, 1785 Massachusetts Ave. N.W., Washington, DC 20036; 202/588-6000; http://www.nthp.org. Especially relevant is the trust's Main Street Center at same address. The center's telephone number is 202/588-6219.

Travel Industry Association, 1100 New York Ave. N.W., Suite 450 West, Washington, DC 20005; 202/408-8422.

Overall Museum Operation

Ambrose, Timothy, and Paine Crispin. *Museum Basics*. London and New York: International Council of Museums and Routledge, 1993.

> This book provides a straightforward discussion of the requirements for operating a museum. The short sections cover visitors, the development and care of the collections, the buildings, the museum's management, and other basics.
>
> *Who should read it?* People with no formal training in museum operations and administrators teaching staff or volunteers how to deal with a particular area. Since the publication is an introductory text, some readers may find it tedious and wonder why the authors cite such common sense actions. But it does provide a vital checklist for successful museum operations as well as helpful tips and suggestions.

George, Gerald and Cindy Sherrell-Leo. *Starting Right: A Basic Guide to Museum Planning*. Nashville: American Association for State and Local History, 1986.

> Its title best describes this easy-to-read book, which provides sensible advice to anyone thinking about starting a museum. It provides criteria for determining whether the proposed museum makes sense, and contains sample documents and lists of other sources.
>
> *Who should read it?* People considering starting a small history museum.

Lord, Gail Dexter and Barry Lord, eds. *The Manual of Museum Planning*. London: HMSO Publications Centre, 1991.

> Written by various experts, the 21 chapters in this manual cover all aspects of planning for and building a museum. Although written for a British audience, the basic material is also useful for people in other countries. The volume describes how to fulfill the needs of museum visitors; market and feasibility analysis; planning for collections management and conservation; safety and security; information management; caring for collections during a building project; the role of the museum director, staff, trustees, and architect in a capital project; design control; cost control; site selection; and adapting an existing building. It provides a thorough and comprehensive approach to creating a museum.
>
> *Who should read it?* Because of its size, detail and cost, this book will be most useful for the director or staff person responsible for creating a new building,

especially if he lacks construction knowledge. Others may refer to a particular chapter, such as the one on security, when seeking in-depth information about a particular topic.

Other publications

Anderson Gail, ed. *Museum Mission Statements: Building a Distinct Identity.* Washington, D.C.: American Association of Museums, 1997.

Crawford, Robert W. *On Board: Guiding Principles for Trustees of Not-For-Profit Organizations.* Santa Fe, N.M.: Western States Arts Federation, 1991.

Cutler, Charlene Perkins. *The Employer's Handbook: A Guide to Personnel Practices and Policies for Museums.* Boston: New England Museum Association, 1996.

Fischer, Daryl K., ed. *Museums, Trustees, and Communities: Building Reciprocal Relationships.* Washington, D.C.: American Association of Museums and Museum Trustee Association, 1997.

Liston, David. *Museum Security and Protection: A Handbook for Cultural Heritage Institutions.* New York: International Council of Museums and Routledge, 1993.

Organizing Your Museum: The Essentials. Washington, D.C.: American Association of Museums, 1989.

Pizer, Laurence R. *A Primer for Local Historical Societies*, 2nd ed. Thousand Oaks, Calif., and Nashville: Altamira Press and the American Association for State and Local History, 1991.

Suggested Guidelines in Museum Security. Arlington, Va: American Society for Industrial Security, 1990.

Tourism

Contact the state department that handles tourism and/or economic development. County and city organizations may have useful data. County and state staff of the Extension Service of the U.S. Department of Agriculture also may provide economic development and tourism data, and there may be experts on staff at local institutions of higher learning.

Calcote, Sharon, Larry Friedman, Sharon Gaiptman, and Robin Roberts. *Rural Tourism Handbook: Selected Case Studies and Development Guide.* Washington, D.C.: U.S. Travel and Tourism Administration, U.S. Department of Commerce, *n.d.*

> This thorough guide provides the basics of organizing and promoting tourism and includes principles, practical advice, and case studies.

> *Who should read it?* Anyone attempting to implement a tourism program.

Green, Joslyn. *Getting Started: How to Succeed in Heritage Tourism.* Washington, D.C.: National Trust for Historic Preservation, Washington, D.C., 1993.

> This pamphlet provides a brief introduction to the importance of heritage as a tourism attraction, principles to consider when developing it, how-to tips, and success stories. The quality of the design, printing, and several excellent photographs make this an attractive public relations piece for heritage tourism.

> *Who should read it?* Its brevity, expense ($25), and visual attractiveness give this pamphlet two possible uses: (1) as a gift to a business person or potential funder whose involvement in a heritage tourism effort would be crucial to its success, or (2) as a gift to a major contributor or volunteer.

Koth, Barbara, Glenn Kreag, and Matthew Robinson, comps. *Q & A About Rural Tourism Development: Based on Audience Questions from the Turn It Around with Tourism Teleconference.* Minneapolis: Minnesota Extension Service, University of Minnesota, 1993.

> This volume provides responses tourism experts gave to questions raised at a national teleconference on tourism. It covers community involvement, politics and tourism, community tourism planning and development, tourism attractions, tourism businesses and services, tourism funding, and tourism marketing. The short comments provide numerous helpful suggestions.

> *Who should read it?* A museum person planning a leadership or other active role in a local tourism effort.

Koth, Barbara, Glenn Kreag, John Sem, and Kathy Kjolhaug. *Rural Tourism Development: Training Guide.* Minneapolis: Minnesota Extension Service, University of Minnesota, 1993.

Rural Development: Tourism Case Studies. St. Paul, Minn.: Educational Development System, 1993. Videotape.

> This outstanding guide provides a step-by-step manual for starting and operating a community tourism effort. Sections cover organization, local

involvement, attractions, community appearance, marketing, funding, and issues in tourism development. It also includes a bibliography. The book, which includes case studies, sample survey forms, and checklists for various tasks, is organized as a training manual, with suggestions for presentation and page layout that would enable a user to create visual aids easily. A companion video presents lengthy case studies of four successful community tourism development, each designed to illustrate a different task: developing attractions, expanding local businesses, identifying and meeting visitor needs, and organizing and funding the project.

Who should read it? Anyone involved in a community tourism project will find this guide useful. Anyone training others or trying to convince people of the potential for their community should obtain both the manual and the video (which is available from Educational Development System, Distribution, Room 3, Coffey Hall, 1420 Eckles Ave., St. Paul, MN 55108).

The Cultural Tourism Handbook. Toronto: Lord Cultural Resources Planning & Management Inc., 1993.

Ontario's Cultural Tourism Product: Technical Appendix. Toronto: Lord Cultural Resources Planning & Management Inc., 1993.

Strategic Directions for Ontario's Cultural Tourism Product. Toronto: Lord Cultural Resources Planning & Management, Inc., 1993.

These three reports were based on a study of cultural tourism in Toronto. Strategic Directions details the findings of the study. The handbook explains how cultural tourism can benefit organizations and communities, and suggests ways to develop it. The appendix contains a brief annotated bibliography and the questionnaires used in the survey.

Who should read them? The handbook provides an overview useful for a board member or business person unlikely to read the full report. Strategic Directions contains information useful for anyone planning a cultural tourism initiative, although much of it focuses on specific data related to Ontario. The appendix includes data useful to an organization or community considering a major study and interested in seeing how one was handled by another group.

Preserving Our Past: Building Our Future. Washington, D.C.: National Trust for Historic Preservation, Heritage Tourism Program, 1995. Videotape.

This 10-minute video provides an overview of heritage tourism, including its contribution to community spirit and tourism.

Who should use it? Those hosting heritage tourism workshops may find it a useful introduction.

Sem, John, et al. *Multi-Cultural Tourism Development.* 4 vols. Denver: The Western Entrepreneurial Network, University of Colorado at Denver, 1994.

Each of these four manuals provides identical basic data about organizing a tourism effort and issues in cultural tourism development, as well as case studies related to one of four ethnic groups: African Americans, Native Americans, Asian Americans, and Hispanic, Chicano, and Latino Americans. The manuals provide good basic data about tourism in a readable form, similar to other books on this list, but perhaps are easier to use. Each manual lists items to consider when working with an ethnic group, suggestions for cultural tourism development, examples, and data on key organizations. The short case studies also indicate people to contact for further information. Videos illustrating successful case examples can be purchased separately.

Who should read it? Anyone actively involved in organizing a tourism effort or desiring a quick overview of major issues involving cultural tourism efforts with minority groups.

Community Travel Development Manual. Atlanta: Southeast Tourism Society, *n.d.*

This short booklet provides good advice on why communities should develop tourism projects, and how to organize local residents in the effort. Much of this information is covered in more detailed form in other manuals. However, the suggestions for developing a sample marketing plan, extending a visitor's stay, and holding a hospitality training conference are excellent.

Who should read it? Anyone in charge of a tourism effort will find this booklet worthwhile. It also can serve as an introduction to the subject for a committee or busy individuals unlikely to read more detailed approaches.

Weaver, Glenn D. *Tourism Development: A Guideline for Rural Communities.* Columbia, Mo.: University Extension, Department of Parks, Recreation, and Tourism, University of Missouri, 1993.

This very readable book explains how to design and implement a tourism program in a rural area. It includes the following topics: assessing your potential, getting started, costs, benefits, analysis of information, planning steps, management, leadership, data collection and monitoring, product development, community education, marketing, and evaluation. The book also provides a reading list and sample forms taking inventory of community attractions and services.

Who should read it? Anyone desiring a quick introduction to tourism development. It is especially appropriate for museum board members. Anyone responsible for implementing such programs should consult more detailed materials on the specific subjects.

Tourism USA Guidelines for Tourism Development: Appraising Tourism Potential, Planning for Tourism, Assessing Product and Market, Marketing Tourism, Visitor Services, Sources of Assistance. Columbia, Mo.: The University of Missouri, Department of Recreation and Park Administration, 1986.

This manual explains how to assess a community's potential for tourism, plan for its development, and implement and market a tourism program. The project director, Glenn Weaver, wrote *Tourism Development: A Guideline for Rural Communities* (cited above). It explains how to measure visitor expenditures and calculate their income multiplier; contains numerous sample forms, including questionnaires, inventories, and evaluation forms; covers the many tasks needed to conduct a program; and provides sources for additional information and financial support.

Who should read it? The individual(s) responsible for the overall program. The book does not lend itself to a straight read-through. Instead, it serves as a reference for specific aspects of programs. Anyone conducting a tourism program or working on a tourism committee will find something useful here.

Wisconsin's Tourism Development Handbook. Madison, Wis.: Wisconsin Division of Tourism, 1992.

Although the first section of this handbook describes services available in Wisconsin, the rest is a short, very readable, and sensible description of the steps any community needs to take to develop a tourism program. It includes information on how to develop hospitality efforts, marketing strategies, and attractions; organizing an event, and familiarization and press tours.

Who should read it? Any museum person working on a community tourism committee that lacks tourism experience will find assistance in this booklet.

Other publications

Cultural Tourism in the United States: A Position Paper for the White House Conference on Travel and Tourism. Washington, D.C.: American Association of Museums, 1995.

Museum Management

Carver, John. *Boards that Make a Difference: A New Design for Leadership in Nonprofit and Public Organizations.* San Francisco: Jossey-Bass Publishers, 1990.

This publication focuses on making nonprofit boards effective. It provides approaches for shifting board attention away from micro-management of operations to creating vision, developing and overseeing policy, identifying values for organizational direction and management, separating board and staff responsibilities, and creating systems for accountability for both board and staff. It identifies many of the pitfalls and difficulties of nonprofit boards and their operations and suggests ways to resolve these problems.

Who should read it? Any museum director dissatisfied with both the way his board is functioning and the relationship between staff and board. New museum directors, directors of new museums, or institutions expanding from a mostly volunteer operation to a larger enterprise, will find it helpful. It also can provide orientation for new board members, and encourage reconsideration of the board's current approaches. A museum director might share sections with some staff members.

Kuyper, Joan. *Volunteer Program Administration: A Handbook for Museums and Other Cultural Institutions.* New York: American Council for the Arts, 1993.

The genesis of this excellent manual was a roundtable on volunteerism and trusteeship in the arts, which included participants from the American Association for Museum Volunteers, American Association of Museums, and American Council for the Arts. It covers every aspect of employing museum volunteers: identifying possible jobs; developing and administering an effective program; and recruiting, selecting, training, evaluating, and rewarding volunteers. Each section contains examples from museums, such as a supervisor's evaluation form used at Mystic Seaport, Mystic, Conn. A 41-page "Resource and Networking Guide" provides data on organizations and museums with expertise in volunteer management, as well as a list of helpful written materials.

Who should read it? Any museum administrator using or contemplating using volunteers. Any volunteer with supervisory responsibility. Board members unfamiliar with the work involved in establishing and operating an effective volunteer effort.

Other publications

Barry, Bryan W. *Strategic Planning Workbook for Nonprofit Organizations.* St. Paul, Minn.: Amherst H. Wilder Foundation, 1986.

Bergman, Jed I. *Managing Change in the Nonprofit Sector.* San Francisco: Jossey-Bass, Inc., Publishers, 1996.

Eadie, Douglas C. *Beyond Strategic Planning: How to Involve Nonprofit*

Boards in Growth and Change. Washington, D.C.: National Center for Nonprofit Boards, 1993.

Lord, Barry, and Gail Dexter Lord. *The Manual of Museum Management.* London: The Stationery Office, 1997.

Moore, Kevin, ed. *Museum Management.* New York: Routledge, 1994.

Wolf, Thomas. *Managing a Nonprofit Organization.* Englewood Cliffs, N.J.: Prentice Hall, 1990.

Exhibits

Ambrose, Timothy and Crispin Paine. *Museum Basics.* London and New York: International Council of Museums and Routledge, 1993.

Units 17 through 29 cover exhibit design and creation, including interpretation, presentation techniques, lighting, showcases, planning a new display, research for displays, writing text, briefing a designer, exhibit design and production, and evaluation of exhibitions. Each short section covers the basics and provides insightful tips. The sections on security, conservation, and oral history are particularly helpful.

Who should read it? A good basic introduction useful for the beginner or as a checklist for those with more experience. In terms of exhibits, the coverage is less thorough than Arminta Neal's books (cited below) and does not provide construction data. It does, however, provide tips and material on basic museum operations not included in Neal's books.

Neal, Arminta. *Exhibits for the Small Museum: A Handbook.* Nashville: American Association of State and Local History, 1976.

_____. *Help for the Small Museum: Handbook of Exhibit Ideas and Methods,* 2nd ed. Boulder, Colo.: Pruett Publishing Company, 1987.

Both books provide excellent, clear information. The first covers basic design and construction of exhibits including scale models, case interiors, lighting, mannikins, labels, and museum fatigue. Numerous drawings and photographs clarify the points.

The latter book includes every aspect of basic exhibit design and construction, from conceptualization—telling the story—to installing a fluorescent light fixture. Topics covered under general principles include: the planning process, gallery design, corridors, exhibit cases, panels, color and light, labels, and dealing with problematical items such as firearms, farm implements, and period rooms. Neal provides clear and sensible suggestions, with photographs or drawings of good and bad examples. The second half of the book covers tools, materials, panel and case construction, wiring and installing light fixtures, labels, and finishing methods. Neal assumes that the reader has no prior construction knowledge, and starts with pictures and descriptions of basic hand and power tools. The book includes such practical advice as "do not assume, because you have ordered 8-foot lengths, that all boards will be [that] length. Many boards will be at least 1/4-inch longer. . . . Never assume board ends are square. . . . Always check the ends with [a] combination square." The appendix explains how to keep records, and lists additional resources and publications. And the regional conservation centers listed on page 172 of *Help for the Small Museum* will provide advice on protecting exhibition objects.

Who should read them? Although most readers will want to use *Help for the Small Museum*, the layperson looking for help in planning or constructing exhibits will find either book useful. Students, interns, volunteers, and those who direct them will find these books especially helpful. Even experienced exhibits developers might refer to some sections when working with less experienced helpers. Some material in *Exhibits for the Small Museum* is not contained in the later book, including an entire section on mannikins

Walsh, Amy, ed. *Insights: Museums, Visitors, Attitudes, Expectations: A Focus Group Experiment.* Los Angeles: The J. Paul Getty Trust and the Getty Center for Education in the Arts, 1991.

This excellent publication summarizes the findings from focus group studies at 11 art galleries around the nation. It also includes commentary from a colloquium on the focus group effort, data on the methodology used, and quotes from focus group participants. A companion video is available.

Who should read it? Anyone concerned with conducting focus groups or improving their museum.

Other publications

Ames, Kenneth L., Barbara Franco, and L. Thomas Frye. *Ideas and Images: Developing Interpretive History Exhibits.* Thousand Oaks, Calif., and Nashville: Altamira Press and the American Association of State and Local History, 1992.

Belcher, Michael. *Exhibitions in Museums.* Washington, D.C.: Smithsonian Institution Press, 1992.

Blais, Andrée. *Text in the Exhibition Medium.* Québec City, Canada: La Societé des Musées Québécois, 1995.

Dean, David. *Museum Exhibition: Theory and Practice.* New York: Routledge, 1997.

Kennedy, Jeff. *User Friendly: Hands-On Exhibits That Work*. Washington, D.C.: Association of Science-Technology Centers, 1990.

McLean, Kathleen. *Planning for People in Museum Exhibitions*. Washington, D.C.: Association of Science-Technology Centers, 1993.

Standards Manual for Signs and Labels. Washington, D.C. and New York: American Association of Museums and the Metropolitan Museum of Art, 1995.

Take to the Streets: Guide to Planning Outdoor, Public Exhibits. Flushing Meadows, N.Y.: New York Hall of Science, 1995.

Witteborg, Lothar P. *Good Show! A Practical Guide for Temporary Exhibitions*, 2nd ed. Washington, D.C.: Smithsonian Institution Traveling Exhibition Service, 1991.

Other sources

American Association of Museums, 1575 Eye St. N.W., Washington, D.C. 20005.

Museum Reference Center, Center for Museum Studies, Smithsonian Institution, 900 Jefferson Dr. S.W., Room 2235, Smithsonian Institution, Washington, DC 20560. The Museum Reference Center has an extensive bibliography on exhibits.

American Association for State and Local History, 530 Church Street, Suite 600, Nashville, TN 37219. The AASLH has published books and a series of technical leaflets dealing with exhibits.

Oral History

Baum, Willa K. *Oral History for the Local Historical Society,* 3rd ed. Nashville: American Association for State and Local History, 1987.

> This book explains how to organize an oral history program. It includes choosing both subject and interviewer, conducting the interviews, deciding on equipment and tapes, indexing, transcribing, preserving tapes, permissions, and ethics. It also includes an annotated bibliography of manuals and books on oral history, and examples of its use.

> *Who should read it?* Museum staff involved in oral history efforts. Anyone supervising or training students or volunteers conducting oral history interviews.

Other sources

Oral History Association, P.O. Box 926, University Station, Lexington, KY 40506-0025. The association holds workshops, conducts an annual meeting, and publishes both a quarterly newsletter and an annual review with longer articles.

Diversity

Hopper, Gena Kwon, ed. *Action Plan: Multicultural Initiatives in Texas Museums.* Austin, Tex.: Texas Association of Museums, 1995.

> This outstanding short publication, developed by a committee of the Texas Association of Museums, provides principles, step-by-step recommendations, case studies, and examples for creating a multicultural museum. The writers, clearly experts, address complex issues in an extraordinarily sensitive manner and provide specific suggestions about how to proceed. A glossary of terms commonly used to describe racial and ethnic differences addresses the fact that "many people are uncertain about which terms are appropriate and feel uncomfortable about seeking additional information." A list of community resources includes a variety of local, state and national organizations. The short bibliography lists books dealing with diversity; African-American, Asian, Hispanic, Judaic, Middle Eastern, and Native American cultures; women; and general reference material. The books include scholarly works, fiction, and autobiographical works written over the past 30 years.

> *Who should read it?* Any museum professional, board member, or volunteer concerned with diversity. Those concerned with marketing to a diverse audience and in developing partnerships with minority groups will find it extremely useful.

Other publications

Bay Area Research Project: Multicultural Audience Study for Bay Area Museums. San Francisco: Museum Management Consultants, Inc., 1994.

DiMaggio, Paul, and Francie Ostrower. *Race, Ethnicity, and Participation in the Arts.* Washington, D.C.: Seven Locks Press, 1993.

Recruiting and Retaining a Diverse Staff. Washington, D.C.: American Association of Museums, 1995.

Rutledge, Jennifer M. *Building Board Diversity.* Washington, D.C.: National Center for Nonprofit Boards, 1994.

Marketing

Standard texts as well as more popular books on marketing have flooded the market. To locate one best suited for your needs, contact a college professor of marketing or business, or browse through publications at a large or college bookstore. Also ask your local librarian about periodicals that publish current data on demographics, marketing, and leisure trends.

Adams, G. Donald. *Museum Public Relations.* Nashville: American Association for State and Local History, 1983.

> Written by the former director of public relations at the Henry Ford Museum & Greenfield Village, Dearborn, Mich., this publication provides thorough and practical advice for developing public relations efforts, including approaches to research and planning, identifying and reaching various audiences, fund raising, providing materials for the media, daily operations, and troubleshooting. The appendix includes examples, primarily from the Henry Ford Museum.
>
> *Who should read it?* No one should be deterred by the fact that this book was published in 1983. Only a small portion of the discussion seems dated; most of the book outlines basic principles and provides how-to suggestions applicable to any museum today. Public relations directors, volunteer supervisors, or any staff with limited public relations experience will find this book extremely useful.

Levinson, Jay Conrad. *Guerrilla Marketing: Secrets for Making Big Profits from Your Small Business.* Boston: Houghton Mifflin Company, 1993.

> In addition to describing standard marketing techniques, Levinson provides suggestions on adapting them for institutions with small budgets. He discusses how to develop a marketing plan, the pros and cons of different media, and ways to save money on each. The book includes tips ranging from words to use when addressing older people to the types of envelopes to use for direct mailings.
>
> *Who should read it?* Any museum director or marketing person who desires more experience will gain from this book. It is especially useful for newcomers to the field or people looking for ways to cut costs.

Other publications

Fitzpatrick, Joyce L. *The Board's Role in Public Relations and Communications.* Washington, D.C.: National Center for Nonprofit Boards, 1993.

Hall, Jason. *How to Be Your Museum's Best Advocate*. Washington, D.C.: American Association of Museums, 1994.

Management Support Services. *Marketing Workbook for Nonprofit Organizations*. St. Paul, Minn.: Amherst H. Wilder Foundation, 1990.

McLeish, Barry J. *Successful Marketing Strategies for Nonprofit Organizations*. New York: John Wiley & Sons, Inc., 1995.

Rafool, Mandy, and Laura Loyacono. *Creative Solutions for Funding the Arts*. Washington, D.C.: National Conference of State Legislatures, 1995.

Steckel, Richard. *Marketing: Money and Profit*. East Dundee, Ill.: Creative Core, 1996. Videotape.

Basic Fund Raising

Flanagan, Joan. *The Grass Roots Fundraising Book: How to Raise Money in Your Community*. Chicago: Contemporary Books, 1992.

_____. *Successful Fundraising: A Complete Handbook for Volunteers and Professionals*. Chicago: Contemporary Books, 1993.

The first reference, a basic step-by-step guide, describes experiences and common-sense solutions from fundraisers for small nonprofit organizations. It covers sources of money, organizing a board or fund-raising committee, and calculating the most cost-effective approaches. It also examines memberships, donors, the general public, bookkeeping, and record keeping, and gives examples of simple and complex fund-raising events. The final chapters provide recommendations for obtaining further advice, bibliographic references, and other resources.

The second book provides a more sophisticated approach to fund raising, including detailed analysis of sources of funds, building a fund-raising team, creating a broad base of support as a pool for larger gifts, locating and approaching major donors, corporate contributions, business ventures, and grants. It also provides suggestions about how to hire fund-raising staff and consultants, all in an informal and readable style.

Who should read them? Its upbeat and informal style make *The Grass Roots Fundraising Book* especially appropriate for a fund-raising newcomer, while more experienced fundraisers may prefer the more detailed approach of *Successful Fundraising*. The straightforward comments in the first book may help to convince reluctant board members or trustees to assume more personal responsibility and to use fund raising as a means to build the organization.

Boards that are trying to end a reliance on government and foundation support will find this book helpful. This book also is appropriate for the board member who feels it is rude to ask for money or that some other organization might need it more.

Museum directors, chairs of the board and fund-raising committee, and anyone seriously dedicated to raising money for the institution will find the second book highly profitable.

Greenfield, James M. *Fund-Raising Fundamentals: A Guide to Annual Giving for Professionals and Volunteers.* New York: John Wiley & Sons, Inc., 1994.

Greenfield provides detailed discussions of recruiting fundraisers, direct mail efforts, donor renewal, memberships, benefits and special events, volunteers, personal contacts and other methods of solicitation, and managing a comprehensive annual giving program. The book provides both overall approaches and details, such as how much the post office charges for returned mail. It includes lists of tasks with time lines and budgets. The appendices provide a six-page master checklist for activities, benefits, and special events, as well as a useful bibliography.

Who should read it? People responsible for fund raising. Its dense style makes it hard to read the entire book, but sections and selected lists and examples will prove valuable to staff or volunteers responsible for a specific activity.

Graham, Christine. *Keep the Money Coming: A Step-by-Step Strategic Guide to Annual Fundraising.* Sarasota, Fla.: Pineapple Press, 1992.

Graham provides clear step-by-step instructions about what to do and what mistakes to avoid. The book covers why people give, planning an annual campaign, personal solicitation, personal mail, direct mail, telephone solicitation, and special events. It discusses raising membership figures, ways to keep volunteers productive and morale high, and addresses how to encourage reluctant board members to solicit donations. Graham also explains how to select a computer system, and includes short sections on capital campaigns, endowment drives, bequests, planned gifts, grants, and a short bibliography.

Who should read it? People involved in all aspects of fund raising will find this publication useful.

Iley, Sarah J.E. *Befriending Museums: A Handbook.* Toronto: The Council for Business and Arts in Canada, 1995.

Published in both English and French, this short publication contains many ideas, suitable for smaller museums, about fund raising, membership development, and development of community pride. The illustrations, quotes, and case materials add to its attractiveness.

Who should read it? This book will stimulate ideas among board members and volunteers.

McCarthy, Bridget Beattie. *Cultural Tourism: How the Arts Can Help Market Tourism Products and How Tourism Can Help Provide Markets for the Arts,* 1992. Available from the American Association of Museums.

McCarthy combines an overview of tourism, cultural tourism, and the arts, and their connection to each other, with how-to advice and information about organizations dealing with all three disciplines. The general information on planning and tourism is available elsewhere, but many museums may not be familiar with the various tourism and arts networks. The 30 pages of appendices list historic preservation, cultural conservation, arts creation/presentation, humanities, tourism, and travel organizations. The cartoons are delightful.

Who should read it? This book may serve as a reference for those who want to learn more about cultural tourism and the role that artists can play. Some of the data will help orient newcomers to either tourism or the cultural world, but the small typeface and mass of data make the book difficult to read or skim.

Other publications

Bauer, David G. *The "How To" Grants Manual: Successful Grant Seeking Techniques for Obtaining Public and Private Grants,* 3rd ed. Phoenix: American Council on Education and Oryx Press, 1995.

The Big Book of Museum Grant Money. Washington, D.C.: American Association of Museums, 1995.

Howe, Fisher. *The Board Member's Guide to Fund Raising: What Every Trustee Needs to Know About Raising Money.* San Francisco: Jossey-Bass Inc., Publishers, 1991.

Miner, Lynn E., and Jerry Griffith. *Proposal Planning and Writing.* Phoenix: Oryx Press, 1993.

Reiss, Alvin. *Don't Just Applaud—Send Money!* New York: Theatre Communications Group, 1995.

Rosso, Henry A., and Associates. *Achieving Excellence in Fund Raising: A Comprehensive Guide to Principles, Strategies, and Methods.* San Francisco: Jossey-Bass Inc., Publishers, 1991.

Museum Stores

Increasing Retailer Productivity: A Guide for Shopping Center Profession-als. New York: International Council of Shopping Centers, 1988.

This easy-to-read publication is the most requested item at the library of the Wisconsin State Main Street program. It provides hands-on tips for helping retail stores improve their business from experts, such as successful mall operators, store owners, and consultants. The guide includes data on selecting consultants, displays, use of research, training and motivating employees, and promotion. It contains a 15-page list of resources, including consultants, books, audio-visual materials, periodicals, and organizations.

Who should read it? Operators of museum stores and directors who desire a better understanding of the retail business so that they can become more involved with tourism committees.

Theobald, Mary Miley. *Museum Store Management.* Nashville: American Association for State and Local History, 1991.

According to Theobald, "A true museum store is a hybrid, a cross between a gift shop and a museum exhibit [that contributes to] the institution's stated purposes both financially and educationally." Her book addresses finding a balance between educational mission and earning a profit, and gives specific suggestions on how to maximize both. It provides details about retailing, including designing space, pricing, inventory, merchandising, and protecting the store from theft—helpful information for all museum store staff. Theobald devotes 40 pages to examples of appropriate and profitable product development for museums, with specific recommendations on what to do, sources of crafts people, and how to use the museum's collection for product development in a manner that furthers both the educational and financial objectives. A short, but targeted, annotated bibliography follows the text.

Who should read it? Any director of a small or medium-sized museum who wants to make the museum store more profitable or is searching for ways to create profitable products based on the collection. Any museum store manager, especially one with a retail background but little museum experience, and museum staff or volunteers without considerable retail experience. Larger museums in search of new product ideas or contacts for producing products will find them here. Boards and staff contemplating starting a museum store also will find a great deal of helpful information.

Other publications

The Manager's Guide: Basic Guidelines for the New Manager. Denver: Museum Store Association, 1992.

The New Store Workbook. Denver: Museum Store Association, 1994.

Other sources

Museum Store Association, One Cherry Center, 501 S. Cherry St., Suite 460, Denver, CO 80222; 303/329-6968.

Product Development

Steckel, Dr. Richard, Robin Simons, and Peter Lengsfelder. *Filthy Rich and Other Nonprofit Fantasies: Changing the way nonprofits do business in the 90s*. Berkeley, Calif.: Ten Speed Press, 1989.

Richard Steckel directed the Denver Children's Museum for almost eight years. During that time, he applied entrepreneurial methods, such as product development, to fund raising, eventually obtaining 95 percent of the museum's operating budget through earned revenue. This book explains his philosophy, approaches, and specific techniques, and includes case studies, examples, and how-to information.

Who should read it? A director, board member, or staff member who wants the museum to earn money through non-traditional activities will learn from Steckel's experiences and those of the other nonprofit organizations discussed in the book.

Festivals

Museums sponsor festivals to raise funds, generate publicity and good-will, recruit volunteers and potential members, and market to new audiences. Museum staff may wish to increase their knowledge of festival operation so that they may participate effectively in the production of community festivals.

Beamish, Royd E. *Planning Festivals and Events*. Ottawa, Canada: Canadian Government Office of Tourism, Department of Industry, Trade, and Commerce, 1982.

Partly due to the print size, some will find this book difficult to read. But it does contain detailed information on the various tasks necessary to conduct a successful festival, including organizational development, staffing, committee structures, publicity, accounting, fund raising, and evaluation.

Who should read it? Persons responsible for producing a festival will find tips on what to do and how to do it, as well as lists of tasks for committee chairs.

Committee chairs should read the sections dealing with their areas of
responsibility.

Building a Festival: A Framework for Organizers. Little Rock, Ark.:
Arkansas Department of Parks and Tourism, *n.d.*

This quick, snappy overview provides tips on producing a festival, including
choosing a theme and a name, organizational development, publicity, making
money, food, arts and crafts activities, children's activities, physical logistics,
and case studies.

Who should read it? Anyone considering putting on a festival or a similar
event. The book does not provide detailed lists of tasks like the Beamish book,
but it is easier to read and more likely to stimulate ideas.

Festivals and Events. St. Paul, Minn.: Minnesota Office of Tourism, Minnesota Extension Service Small Business Development Center, University of Minnesota, 1989.

This loose-leaf notebook contains reprints of articles, speeches, and handouts.
It includes story boarding (a planning technique), a festival planning
handbook, and materials on publicity, such as tips on writing public service
announcements. Some of the individual items are quite good, but much of the
material is available elsewhere.

Who should read it? This collection of articles is useful both for someone
inexperienced in fund raising and for more experienced fund raisers looking
for some helpful hints.